THE ROOTS OF ROMANTICISM

Isaiah Berlin was born in Riga, capital of Latvia, in 1909. When he was six, his family moved to Russia: there in 1917, in Petrograd, he witnessed both the Social Democratic and the Bolshevik Revolution.

In 1921 his family came to England, and he was educated at St Paul's School and Corpus Christi College, Oxford. At Oxford he was a Fellow of All Souls, a Fellow of New College, Professor of Social and Political Theory and founding President of Wolfson College. He also held the Presidency of the British Academy. His published work includes *Karl Marx, Four Essays on Liberty, Russian Thinkers, Concepts and Categories, Against the Current, Personal Impressions, The Crooked Timber of Humanity, The Sense of Reality, The Proper Study of Mankind, The Power of Ideas* and *Three Critics of the Enlightenment*. As an exponent of the history of ideas he was awarded the Erasmus, Lippincott and Agnelli Prizes; he also received the Jerusalem Prize for his lifelong defence of civil liberties. He died in 1997.

Dr Henry Hardy, a Fellow of Wolfson College, Oxford, is one of Isaiah Berlin's Literary Trustees. He has edited several other books by Berlin, and is currently preparing his letters and his remaining unpublished writings for publication.

For further information about Isaiah Berlin visit
www.wolfson.ox.ac/berlin/vl/

The A. W. Mellon Lectures
in the Fine Arts

The National Gallery of Art
Washington, D.C.
Bollingen Series xxxv:45

Also by Isaiah Berlin

✻

KARL MARX
THE AGE OF ENLIGHTENMENT
FOUR ESSAYS ON LIBERTY

Edited by Henry Hardy and Aileen Kelly
RUSSIAN THINKERS

Edited by Henry Hardy
CONCEPTS AND CATEGORIES
AGAINST THE CURRENT
PERSONAL IMPRESSIONS
THE CROOKED TIMBER OF HUMANITY
THE SENSE OF REALITY
THE POWER OF IDEAS
THREE CRITICS OF THE ENLIGHTENMENT

Edited by Henry Hardy and Roger Hausheer
THE PROPER STUDY OF MANKIND

THE ROOTS OF ROMANTICISM

The A. W. Mellon Lectures
in the Fine Arts
The National Gallery of Art,
Washington, D.C.
Bollingen Series xxxv:45

ISAIAH BERLIN

Edited by Henry Hardy

Princeton University Press
Princeton, New Jersey

Published in North America by Princeton University Press,
41 William Street, Princeton, New Jersey 08540
Published in Great Britain by Chatto & Windus Ltd

This is the forty-fifth volume of the A. W. Mellon Lectures in the Fine Arts,
which are delivered annually at the National Gallery of Art, Washington.
The volumes of lectures constitute Number xxxv in Bollingen Series,
sponsored by Bollingen Foundation.

Third printing, and first paperback printing, 2001
Paperback ISBN 0–691–08662–1

The Library of Congress has cataloged the cloth edition of this book as follows

Berlin, Isaiah, Sir.
The roots of romanticism / Isaiah Berlin : edited by Henry Hardy.
p.   cm. — (The A. W. Mellon lectures in the fine arts)
(Bollingen series ; xxxv:45)
First publication of the 1965 A. W. Mellon lectures in the fine arts.
Includes bibliographical references and index.
ISBN 0–691–00713–6 (cl : alk. paper)
1. Romanticism in art.   2. Arts, Modern—18th century.   I. Hardy,
Henry.   II. Title.   III. Series: The A. W. Mellon lectures in the fine arts;
1965.   IV. Series: Bollingen series: xxxv:45.
NX452.5.R64B47   1999
141'.6—dc21   98–41657

This book has been composed in 11/13.5pt Garamond

Printed on acid-free paper. ∞

www.pup.princeton.edu

Printed in the United States of America

9   10

ISBN-13: 978-0-691-08662-0

ISBN-10: 0-691-08662-1

For Alan Bullock

CONTENTS

EDITOR'S PREFACE

Every thing is what it is, and not another thing.

Joseph Butler[1]

Everything is what it is ...

Isaiah Berlin[2]

BUTLER'S REMARK was among Isaiah Berlin's favourite quotations, and Berlin echoes it in one of his most important essays. I take it as my starting-point here because the first thing to be said about the present volume, in order to dispel any possible misunderstanding, is that it is not in any degree the new work on romanticism Berlin had hoped to write ever since giving the (unscripted) A. W. Mellon Lectures on this subject, in March and April 1965, at the National Gallery of Art in Washington. In the years that followed, especially after his retirement from the Presidency of Wolfson College, Oxford, in 1975, he continued to read widely with a book on romanticism in mind, and a large mass of notes accumulated. In the last decade of his life he collected all his notes together in a separate room and started afresh on the task of pulling them together: he made a list of headings and began dictating on to cassette a selection of the notes, marshalling them under the headings as he went. He also considered using his

---

[1] *Fifteen Sermons Preached at the Rolls Chapel*, 2nd ed., 'To which is added a PREFACE' (London, 1729), preface, p. xxix.

[2] 'Two Concepts of Liberty' (1958): p. 197 in *The Proper Study of Mankind: An Anthology of Essays* (London, 1997; New York, 1998).

material as a long introduction to an edition of work by E. T. A. Hoffmann rather than as a free-standing study of his own. But the new synthesis continued to elude him, perhaps partly because he had left it too late, and so far as I am aware not so much as a sentence of the intended work was ever written.

Clearly it is a matter of great regret for his readers, as it certainly was for Berlin himself, that he did not write his revised account. But its absence is not all loss: had it been written, the present book, which is simply an edited transcript of the lectures, would never have been published; and there is a freshness and immediacy, an intensity and excitement in the transcript that would inevitably have been obscured, to some extent, in a carefully reworked and expanded version. There are several other unscripted lectures delivered by Berlin that survive as recordings or transcripts, and some of these can be directly compared either with published texts that derive from them, or with previously composed texts on which they are based. Such a comparison shows how the repeated revisions Berlin tended to undertake on the road to publication, for all that they enrich the intellectual content and precision of a work, can sometimes have a sobering effect on the extempore spoken word; or, conversely, it shows how a long underlying text – a 'torso' as Berlin called it – can acquire new life and directness when used as a source for a lecture not read from a prepared script. The lecture delivered from notes and the carefully constructed book are, one might say in pluralist terminology, incommensurable. In this case, for better or worse, only the former incarnation of one of Berlin's central intellectual projects is available.

The title I have used is one Berlin himself suggested at an early stage. It was supplanted by 'Sources of Romantic Thought' for the delivery of the lectures because in the opening pages of Saul Bellow's novel *Herzog*, published in 1964, the hero, a Jewish academic called Moses Herzog who is undergoing a crisis of self-confidence, is struggling unsuccessfully to deliver a course of adult-education lectures in a New York night-school – lectures entitled precisely 'The Roots of Romanticism'. As far as I know this was a coincidence – Berlin himself certainly denied any direct connection – but, however this may be, the earlier title was certainly more resonant, and if there were any grounds for abandoning it at the time, they have by now surely disappeared.[1]

Even if Berlin's introductory remarks before he began the lectures proper are too occasional to appear in the body of the published text, they remain of some prefatory interest. Here, accordingly, is the greater part of them:

> These lectures are primarily intended for genuine experts on the arts – art historians and experts on aesthetics, amongst whom I cannot possibly count myself. My only valid excuse for choosing this subject is that the romantic movement, naturally, is relevant to the arts: the arts, even though I know not very much about them, cannot be altogether kept out, and I promise not to keep them out beyond measure.
>
> There is a sense in which the connection between romanticism and the arts is even stronger. If I can claim any qualification for talking about this subject, it is because I propose to deal with political and social life, and moral life as well; and it is true, I think, to say of the romantic movement that it is not only a movement in which the arts are concerned, not only an artistic movement, but perhaps the first moment, certainly in the history of the West, when the arts dominated other aspects of life, when there was a kind of tyranny of art over life, which in some sense is the essence of the romantic movement; at least, I propose to try to demonstrate that this is so.
>
> I should add that the interest of romanticism is not simply historical. A great many phenomena of the present day – nationalism, existentialism, admiration for great men, admiration for impersonal institutions, democracy, totalitarianism – are profoundly affected by the rise of romanticism, which enters them all. For this reason it is a subject not altogether irrelevant even to our own day.

Also of some interest is the following fragment, which appears to be a draft opening of the lectures proper, written before they

---

[1] Other titles considered by Berlin include 'Prometheus: A Study of the Rise of Romanticism in the Eighteenth Century' (mentioned only satirically and immediately rejected), 'The Rise of Romanticism', 'The Romantic Impact', 'The Romantic Rebellion', 'The Romantic Revolt' and 'The Romantic Revolution'.

were delivered. It is the only piece of prose composed by Berlin for this project that I have found among his notes:

> I do not propose even to attempt to define romanticism in terms of attributes or purposes, for, as Northrop Frye wisely warns, if one attempts to point to some obvious characteristic of romantic poets – for example, the new attitude to nature or to the individual – and to say that this is confined to the new writers of the period from 1770 to 1820, and to contrast it with the attitude of Pope or Racine, someone is bound to produce contrary instances from Plato or Kalidasa, or (like Kenneth Clark) from the Emperor Hadrian, or (like Seillière) from Heliodorus, or from a medieval Spanish poet or pre-Islamic Arab verse, and finally from Racine and Pope themselves.
>
> Nor do I wish to imply that there are *pure* cases – a sense in which any artist or thinker or person could be said to be *wholly* romantic, and nothing else at all, any more than a man could be said to be *wholly* individual, that is to say, to share no properties with anything else in the world, or *wholly* social, that is to say, to possess no properties unique to himself. Nevertheless, these words are not meaningless, and indeed we cannot do without them: they indicate attributes or tendencies or ideal types the application of which serves to throw light, to identify and perhaps, if they had not been sufficiently noticed earlier, to exaggerate what, for want of a better word, have to be called *aspects* of a man's character, or of his activity, or of an outlook, or of a movement, or of a doctrine.
>
> To say of someone that he is a romantic thinker or a romantic hero is not to say nothing. Sometimes it is to say that what he is or does requires to be explained in terms of a purpose, or a cluster of purposes (perhaps internally contradictory), or a vision, or perhaps glimpses or intimations, which may point towards some state or activity that is in principle unrealisable – something in life or a movement or a work of art which is part of its essence, but not explained, perhaps unintelligible. No more than this has been the purpose of most serious writers on the many – the countless – aspects of romanticism.
>
> My intention is even more limited. It appears to me that a radical shift of values occurred in the latter half of the eighteenth century – before what is properly called the romantic movement – which has affected thought, feeling and action in the Western world. This shift is most vividly expressed in much of what seems to be most characteristically romantic in the romantics: not in all that is romantic in them, nor in what is romantic in all of them, but in something quintessential,

something without which neither the revolution of which I intend to speak, nor those consequences of it recognised by all those who have acknowledged that there was such a phenomenon as the romantic movement – romantic art, romantic thought – would have been possible. If I am told that I have not included the characteristic that lies at the heart of this or that or even every manifestation of romanticism, the case is made – I assent only too readily. It is not my purpose to define romanticism, only to deal with the revolution of which romanticism, at any rate in some of its guises, is the strongest expression and symptom. No more than this: but this is a great deal, for I hope to show that this revolution is the deepest and most lasting of all changes in the life of the West, no less far-reaching than the three great revolutions whose impact is not questioned – the industrial in England, the political in France, and the social and economic in Russia – with which, indeed, the movement with which I am concerned is connected at every level.

In editing the transcripts of these lectures (in the light of the BBC recordings) I have tried to restrict myself, on the whole, to making the minimum changes necessary to ensure a smoothly readable text; I have regarded the informality of style and the occasional mild unorthodoxy of idiom that are natural in lectures given from notes as assets to be preserved, within certain limits. Even though a good deal of syntactic repair-work was sometimes required, as is normal in most transcripts of spontaneously uttered sentences, there is rarely any real doubt about Berlin's intended meaning. A few minor alterations made to the transcripts by Berlin at an earlier stage have been incorporated, and this explains some of the few substantive discrepancies that will be noticed by a reader who, with this book in hand as a libretto, listens to the recordings of the lectures that are available.[1]

I have as always done my best to trace Berlin's quotations, and have made any necessary corrections in what were clearly intended as passages quoted verbatim from an English source, or as direct

---

[1] Berlin's highly individual and arresting manner of delivery has been a central ingredient in his reputation, and the experience of listening to him lecturing is highly recommended. The whole series may be heard (by prior appointment) at the National Gallery of Art in Washington, DC, or at the National Sound Archive in the British Library in London.

translations from another language, rather than as paraphrase. There is, however, another device in Berlin's armoury, intermediate between verbatim quotation and paraphrase, that might be called 'semi-quotation'. The semi-quoted words are sometimes presented between quotation marks, but they have the character of what an author might say, or what he in effect said, rather than claiming to reproduce (or translate) his actual published words. This is a familiar phenomenon in books written before our own time,[1] but has perhaps rather fallen from favour in the contemporary academic climate. In the collections of Berlin's essays that I published in Berlin's lifetime I usually confined myself to direct quotation, checked against a primary source, or overt paraphrase. In a book of this kind, however, it seemed artificial and unduly intrusive to attempt to conceal this perfectly natural and rhetorically effective

[1] Though it is hard to distinguish it from a straightforward lack of the intention to be accurate by today's standards. As Theodore Besterman puts it in the introduction to his translation of Voltaire's *Philosophical Dictionary* (Harmondsworth, 1971, p. 14), 'modern notions of textual fidelity were unknown in the eighteenth century. The words Voltaire places within quotation marks are not always accurate or even direct quotations.' In Giambattista Vico's case matters were even worse, as Thomas Goddard Bergin and Max Harold Fisch record in the preface to a revised edition of their translation of Vico's *New Science* (New York, 1968, pp. v–vi): 'Vico quotes inexactly from memory; his references are vague; his memory is often not of the original source but of a quotation from it in some secondary work; he ascribes to one author what is said by another, or to one work what is said in another by the same author . . .'. However, as Bergin and Fisch put it in the preface to the first edition of their translation (New York, 1948, p. viii), 'A complete exposure of Vico's errors ... would not touch the heart of his argument.'

In Berlin's case, at any rate, there is the further problem that, to the extent that his quotations are not strictly accurate, they are usually improvements on the original. He and I often discussed this, and he was delightfully self-mocking about it, but usually insisted on correction once the facts were established, even though his relaxed approach to quotation almost never distorted the quoted author's meaning, and sometimes clarified it. Of course, the remarks made about Vico by Bergin and Fisch are an enormous exaggeration if applied to Berlin, though, since Vico was one of Berlin's intellectual heroes, the (very partial) analogy has a certain resonance. However, Bergin and Fisch aptly point out (1968, p. vi) that Fausto Nicolini, Vico's famous editor, treats Vico's scholarly shortcomings 'with chastening love' – surely an exemplary editorial attitude.

middle way by insisting that quotation marks should be used only for exact quotation. I mention this so that the reader is not misled, and as background to some further remarks about Berlin's quotations that I make at the beginning of the list of references (p. 148).

The lectures were broadcast by the BBC on its Third Programme in August and September 1966, and again in October and November 1967. They were repeated in 1975 in Australia, and in Britain, on BBC Radio 3, in 1989, the year that Berlin reached the age of eighty. Excerpts have also been included in later programmes about Berlin's work.

Berlin himself steadfastly refused to allow the publication of this transcript in his lifetime, not only because until the last years of his life he still hoped to write the 'proper' book, but also, perhaps, because he believed that it was an act of vanity to publish a straight transcript of unscripted lectures without undertaking the labour of revision and expansion. He was well aware that some of what he had said was probably too general, too speculative, too crude – acceptable from the podium, maybe, but not on the printed page. Indeed, in a letter of thanks to P. H. Newby, then head of BBC Radio's Third Programme, he describes himself as 'letting loose this huge stream of words – more than six hours of hectic, in places incoherent, hurried, breathless – to my ears sometimes hysterical – talk'.[1]

There are those who believe that this transcript should not be published even now – that for all its undoubted interest it will devalue the currency of Berlin's *oeuvre*. With this view I disagree, and I derive support from the opinions of a number of scholars whose judgement I respect, in particular the late Patrick Gardiner, the most fastidious of critics, who read the edited transcript some years ago and voted unequivocally for its publication as it stood. Even if it is indeed a mistake to publish material of this kind in its author's lifetime (and I am ambivalent even about that), it seems to me not only acceptable but highly desirable to do so when the author is as remarkable and the lectures as stimulating as in this case. Besides, Berlin himself clearly accepted that the transcript would be published after his death, and referred to this eventuality without

[1] Letter dated 20 September 1966.

indicating that he had serious reservations. Posthumous publication, he believed, is governed by criteria quite different from those that apply in an author's lifetime; and he must have known, though he would never admit it, that his Mellon Lectures were a *tour de force* of the extempore lecturer's art that deserved to be made permanently available, warts and all. It is now time for this view – to quote his own words about his avowedly controversial book on J. G. Hamann – 'to be accepted or refuted by the critical reader'.[1]

I have a number of debts of gratitude that I should record – more, no doubt, than I can remember. Those concerning the provision of references I mention on p. 150. Otherwise my main obligations (mostly the same as in the case of earlier volumes) are to the most generous benefactors who have financed my Fellowship at Wolfson College; to Lord Bullock for ensuring that I have benefactors to thank; to Wolfson College for housing me and my work; to Pat Utechin, the author's secretary, who has now been my patient friend and supporter for some twenty-five years; to Roger Hausheer and the late Patrick Gardiner for reading and advising on the transcript, and for many other forms of indispensable aid; to Jonny Steinberg for some valuable editorial suggestions; to the publishers who have to withstand my many and exacting requirements, especially Will Sulkin and Rowena Skelton-Wallace at Chatto and Windus, and Deborah Tegarden at Princeton University Press; to Samuel Guttenplan for moral support and useful advice; and finally (though I have thoughtlessly not mentioned them before) to my family for enduring the rather strange form of single-mindedness that underlies my chosen occupation. I hope it is almost superfluous to add that my greatest debt is to Isaiah Berlin himself for entrusting me with the most fulfilling task that an editor could possibly hope for, and for giving me a completely free hand in performing it.

Wolfson College, Oxford   HENRY HARDY
May 1998

[1] From the foreword written specially in 1994 for the German edition of *The Magus of the North*: see Isaiah Berlin, *Der Magus in Norden* (Berlin, 1995), p. 14. [The original English text of this foreword has now been published in Berlin's *Three Critics of the Enlightenment: Vico, Hamann, Herder* (London and Princeton, 2000): for this remark see p. 252 in that volume.]

1

IN SEARCH OF A DEFINITION

I MIGHT be expected to begin, or to attempt to begin, with some kind of definition of romanticism, or at least some generalisation, in order to make clear what it is that I mean by it. I do not propose to walk into that particular trap. The eminent and wise Professor Northrop Frye points out that whenever anyone embarks on a generalisation on the subject of romanticism, even something so innocuous, for example, as to say that a new attitude sprang up among English poets towards nature – in Wordsworth and Coleridge, let us say, as against Racine and Pope – somebody will always be found who will produce countervailing evidence from the writings of Homer, Kalidasa, pre-Muslim Arabian epics, medieval Spanish verse – and finally Racine and Pope themselves. For this reason I do not propose to generalise, but to convey in some other way what it is that I think romanticism to be.

Indeed, the literature on romanticism is larger than romanticism itself, and the literature defining what it is that the literature on romanticism is concerned with is quite large in its turn. There is a kind of inverted pyramid. It is a dangerous and a confused subject, in which many have lost, I will not say their senses, but at any rate their sense of direction. It is like that dark cave described by Virgil, where all the footsteps lead in one direction; or the cave of Polyphemus – those who enter it never seem to emerge again. It is therefore with some trepidation that I embark upon the subject.

The importance of romanticism is that it is the largest recent movement to transform the lives and the thought of the Western world. It seems to me to be the greatest single shift in the consciousness of the West that has occurred, and all the other shifts which have occurred in the course of the nineteenth and twentieth centuries appear to me in comparison less important, and at any rate deeply influenced by it.

The history not only of thought, but of consciousness, opinion, action too, of morals, politics, aesthetics, is to a large degree a history of dominant models. Whenever you look at any particular civilisation, you will find that its most characteristic writings and other cultural products reflect a particular pattern of life which those who are responsible for these writings – or paint these paintings, or produce these particular pieces of music – are dominated by. And in order to identify a civilisation, in order to explain what kind of civilisation it is, in order to understand the world in which men of this sort thought and felt and acted, it is important to try, so far as possible, to isolate the dominant pattern which that culture obeys. Consider, for instance, Greek philosophy or Greek literature of the classical age. If you read, say, the philosophy of Plato, you will find that he is dominated by a geometrical or mathematical model. It is clear that his thought operates on lines which are conditioned by the idea that there are certain axiomatic truths, adamantine, unbreakable, from which it is possible by severe logic to deduce certain absolutely infallible conclusions; that it is possible to attain to this kind of absolute wisdom by a special method which he recommends; that there is such a thing as absolute knowledge to be obtained in the world, and if only we can attain to this absolute knowledge, of which geometry, indeed mathematics in general, is the nearest example, the most perfect paradigm, we can organise our lives in terms of this knowledge, in terms of these truths, once and for all, in a static manner, needing no further change; and then all suffering, all doubt, all ignorance, all forms of human vice and folly can be expected to disappear from the earth.

This notion that there is somewhere a perfect vision, and that it needs only a certain kind of severe discipline, or a certain kind of method, to attain to this truth, which is analogous, at any rate, to the cold and isolated truths of mathematics – this notion then affects a great many other thinkers in the post-Platonic age: certainly the Renaissance, which had similar ideas, certainly thinkers like Spinoza, thinkers in the eighteenth century, thinkers in the nineteenth century too, who believed it possible to attain to some kind of, if not absolute, at any rate nearly absolute knowledge, and in terms of this to tidy the world up, to create some kind of rational order, in which tragedy, vice and stupidity, which have caused so much destruction in the past, can at last be avoided by the use of carefully acquired information and the application to it of universally intelligible reason.

This is one kind of model – I offer it simply as an example. These models invariably begin by liberating people from error, from confusion, from some kind of unintelligible world which they seek to explain to themselves by means of a model; but they almost invariably end by enslaving those very same people, by failing to explain the whole of experience. They begin as liberators and end in some sort of despotism.

Let us look at another example – a parallel culture, that of the Bible, that of the Jews at a comparable period. You will find a totally different model dominating, a totally different set of ideas, which would have been unintelligible to the Greeks. The notion from which both Judaism and Christianity to a large degree sprang is the notion of family life, the relations of father and son, perhaps the relations of members of a tribe to one another. Such fundamental relationships – in terms of which nature and life are explained – as the love of children for their father, the brotherhood of man, forgiveness, commands issued by a superior to an inferior, the sense of duty, transgression, sin and therefore the need to atone for it – this whole complex of qualities, in terms of which the whole of the universe is explained by those who created the Bible, and by those who were to a large extent influenced by it, would have been totally unintelligible to the Greeks.

Consider a perfectly familiar psalm, where the psalmist says that 'When Israel went out of Egypt . . . the sea saw it, and fled: Jordan was driven back. The mountains skipped like rams, and the little hills like lambs', and the earth is ordered to 'Tremble . . . at the presence of the Lord.' This would have been totally unintelligible to Plato or to Aristotle, because the whole notion of a world which reacts personally to the orders of the Lord, the idea that all relationships, both animate and inanimate, must be interpreted in terms of the relations of human beings, or at any rate in terms of the relations of personalities, in one case divine, in the other case

3

human, is very remote from the Greek conception of what a God was and what his relations were to mankind. Hence the absence among the Greeks of the notion of obligation, hence the absence of the notion of duty, which it is so difficult for people to grasp who read the Greeks through spectacles partly affected by the Jews.

Let me try to convey how strange different models can be, because this is important simply in tracing the history of these transformations of consciousness. Considerable revolutions have occurred in the general outlook of mankind which it is sometimes difficult to retrace, because we swallow them as if they were familiar. Giambattista Vico – the Italian thinker who flourished at the beginning of the eighteenth century, if a man who was totally poor and neglected may be said to have flourished – was perhaps the first to draw our attention to the strangeness of ancient cultures. He points out, for example, that in the quotation 'Jovis omnia plena' ('Everything is full of Jove'), which is the end of a perfectly familiar Latin hexameter, something is said that to us is not wholly intelligible. On the one hand Jupiter or Jove is a large bearded divinity who hurls thunder and lightning. On the other hand, everything – 'omnia' – is said to be 'full of' this bearded being, which is not on the face of it intelligible. Vico then argues with great imagination and cogency that the view of these ancient peoples, so remote from us, must have been very different from ours for them to have been able to conceive of their divinity not only as a bearded giant commanding the gods and men, but also as something of which the whole heavens could be full.

Let me give a more familiar example. When Aristotle in the *Nicomachean Ethics* discusses the subject of friendship, he says, in what is to us a somewhat surprising manner, that there are various kinds of friends. For example there is the friendship which consists in passionate infatuation by one human being with another; and there is also a friendship which consists in business relations, in trading, in buying and selling. The fact that for Aristotle there is nothing strange in saying there are two kinds of friends, that there are people whose whole lives are given to love, or at any rate whose emotions are passionately engaged in love, and on the other hand there are people who sell shoes to one another, and these are species of the same genus, is something to which, as a result,

perhaps, of Christianity, or of the romantic movement, or whatever it may be, we find it rather difficult to acclimatise ourselves.

I give these examples merely in order to convey that these
ancient cultures are stranger than we think, and that larger
transformations have occurred in the history of human consciousness than an ordinary uncritical reading of the classics would seem
to convey. There are of course a great many other examples. The
world can be conceived organically – like a tree, in which every
part lives for every other part, and through every other part – or
mechanistically, perhaps as a result of some scientific model, in
which the parts are external to one another, and in which the State,
or any other human institution, is regarded as a gadget for the
purpose of promoting happiness, or preventing people from doing
each other in. These are very different conceptions of life, and they
do belong to different climates of opinion, and are influenced by
different considerations.

What happens as a rule is that some subject gains the ascendancy
– say physics, or chemistry – and, as a result of the enormous hold
which it has upon the imagination of its generation, it is applied in
other spheres as well. This happened to sociology in the nineteenth
century, it happened to psychology in our own. My thesis is that
the romantic movement was just such a gigantic and radical
transformation, after which nothing was ever the same. This is the
claim on which I wish to focus.

Where did the romantic movement take its rise? Certainly not in
England, although technically, no doubt, it did – that is what all the
historians will tell you. At any rate, that is not where it occurred in
its most dramatic form. Here the question arises: When I speak of
romanticism, do I mean something which happens historically, as I
appear to be saying, or is it perhaps a permanent frame of mind
which is not exclusive to, is not monopolised by, any particular
age? Herbert Read and Kenneth Clark[1] have taken up the
position that romanticism is a permanent state of mind which
might be found anywhere. Kenneth Clark finds it in some lines of
Hadrian's; Herbert Read quotes a great many examples. The Baron
Seillière, who has written extensively on this subject, quotes Plato

---

[1] Both previous Mellon Lecturers.

and Plotinus and the Greek novelist Heliodorus, and a great many other persons who, in his opinion, were romantic writers. I do not wish to enter upon this issue – it may be so. The subject with which I myself wish to deal is confined in time. I do not wish to deal with a permanent human attitude, but with a particular transformation which occurred historically, and affects us today. Therefore I propose to confine my attention to what occurred in the second third of the eighteenth century. It occurred not in England, not in France, but for the most part in Germany.

The common view of history and historical change gives us this account. We begin with a French *dix-huitième*, an elegant century in which everything begins by being calm and smooth, rules are obeyed in life and in art, there is a general advance of reason, rationality is progressing, the Church is retreating, unreason is yielding to the great attacks upon it of the French *philosophes*. There is peace, there is calm, there is elegant building, there is a belief in the application of universal reason both to human affairs and to artistic practice, to morals, to politics, to philosophy. Then there is a sudden, apparently unaccountable, invasion. Suddenly there is a violent eruption of emotion, enthusiasm. People become interested in Gothic buildings, in introspection. People suddenly become neurotic and melancholy; they begin to admire the unaccountable flight of spontaneous genius. There is a general retreat from this symmetrical, elegant, glassy state of affairs. At the same time other changes occur too. A great revolution breaks out; there is discontent; the King has his head cut off; the Terror begins.

It is not quite clear what these two revolutions have to do with each other. As we read history, there is a general sense that something catastrophic occurred towards the end of the eighteenth century. At first things appeared to go comparatively smoothly, then there was a sudden breakthrough. Some welcome it, some denounce it. Those who denounce it suppose this to have been an elegant and peaceful age: those who did not know it, did not know the true *plaisir de vivre*, as Talleyrand said. Others say it was an artificial and hypocritical age, and that the Revolution ushered in a reign of greater justice, greater humanity, greater freedom, greater understanding of man for man. However that may be, the question is: What is the relation of the so-called romantic revolution – the sudden breakthrough in the realms of art and morals of this new and turbulent attitude – and the revolution which is normally known as the French Revolution? Were the people who danced upon the ruins of the Bastille, the people who cut off the head of Louis XVI, the same persons as those who were affected by the sudden cult of genius, or the sudden breakthrough of emotionalism of which we are told, or the sudden disturbance and turbulence which flooded the Western world? Apparently not. Certainly the principles in the name of which the French Revolution was fought were principles of universal reason, of order, of justice, not at all connected with the sense of uniqueness, the profound emotional introspection, the sense of the differences of things, dissimilarities rather than similarities, with which the romantic movement is usually associated.

What about Rousseau? Rousseau is of course quite correctly assigned to the romantic movement as, in a sense, one of its fathers. But the Rousseau who was responsible for the ideas of Robespierre, the Rousseau who was responsible for the ideas of the French Jacobins, is not the Rousseau, it seems to me, who has an obvious connection with romanticism. That Rousseau is the Rousseau who wrote *The Social Contract*, which is a typically classical treatise that speaks of the return of man to those original, primary principles which all men have in common; the reign of universal reason, which unites men, as opposed to emotions, which divide them; the reign of universal justice and universal peace as against the conflicts and the turbulence and the disturbances which tear human hearts from their minds and divide men against themselves.

So it is difficult to see what the relation is of this great romantic upheaval to the political revolution. Then there is the Industrial Revolution too, which cannot be regarded as irrelevant. After all, ideas do not breed ideas. Some social and economic factors are surely responsible for great upheavals in human consciousness. We have a problem on our hands. There is the Industrial Revolution, there is the great French political revolution under classical auspices, and there is the romantic revolution. Take even the great art of the French Revolution. If, for example, you look at the great revolutionary paintings of David, it is difficult to connect him specifically with the romantic revolution. The paintings of David have a kind of eloquence, the austere Jacobin eloquence of a return to Sparta, a return to Rome; they communicate a protest against the frivolity and the superficiality of life which is connected with the preachings of such men as Machiavelli or Savonarola or Mably, people who denounced the frivolity of their age in the name of eternal ideals of a universal kind, whereas the romantic movement, we are told by all its historians, was a passionate protest against universality of any kind. Therefore there is, prima facie at any rate, a problem in understanding what happened.

In order to give some sense of what I regard this great breakthrough as being, why I think that in those years, say 1760 to 1830, something transforming occurred, that there was a great break in European consciousness – in order to give you at any rate some preliminary evidence of why I think there is even a case for saying this, let me give an example. Suppose you were travelling about Western Europe, say in the 1820s, and suppose you spoke, in France, to the avant-garde young men who were friends of Victor Hugo, *Hugolâtres*. Suppose you went to Germany and spoke there to the people who had once been visited by Madame de Staël, who had interpreted the German soul to the French. Suppose you had met the Schlegel brothers, who were great theorists of romanticism, or one or two of the friends of Goethe in Weimar, such as the fabulist and poet Tieck, or other persons connected with the romantic movement, and their followers in the universities, students, young men, painters, sculptors, who were deeply influenced by the work of these poets, these dramatists, these critics. Suppose you had spoken in England to someone who had been influenced by, say, Coleridge, or above all by Byron – anyone influenced by Byron, whether in England or France or Italy, or beyond the Rhine, or beyond the Elbe. Suppose you had spoken to these persons. You would have found that their ideal of life was approximately of the following kind. The values to which they attached the highest importance were such values as integrity, sincerity, readiness to sacrifice one's life to some inner light, dedication to some ideal for which it is worth sacrificing all that one is, for which it is worth both living and dying. You would have found that they were not primarily interested in knowledge, or in the advance of science, not interested in political power, not interested in happiness, not interested, above all, in adjustment to life, in finding your place in society, in living at peace with your government, even in loyalty to your king, or to your republic. You would have found that common sense, moderation, was very far from their thoughts. You would have found that they believed in the necessity of fighting for your beliefs to the last breath in your body, and you would have found that they believed in the value of martyrdom as such, no matter what the martyrdom was martyrdom for. You would have found that they believed that minorities were more holy than majorities, that failure was nobler than success, which had something shoddy and something vulgar about it. The very notion of idealism, not in its philosophical sense, but in the ordinary sense in which we use it, that is to say the state of mind of a man who is prepared to sacrifice a great deal for principles or for some conviction, who is not prepared to sell out, who is prepared to go to the stake for something which he believes, because he believes in it – this attitude was relatively new. What people admired was wholeheartedness, sincerity, purity of soul, the ability and readiness to dedicate yourself to your ideal, no matter what it was.

No matter what it was: that is the important thing. Suppose you had a conversation in the sixteenth century with somebody fighting in the great religious wars which tore Europe apart at that period, and suppose you said to a Catholic of that period, engaged in hostilities, 'Of course these Protestants believe what is false; of course to believe what they believe is to court perdition; of course they are dangerous to the salvation of human souls, than which there is nothing more important; but they are so sincere, they die so readily for their cause, their integrity is so splendid, one must yield a certain meed of admiration for the moral dignity and sublimity of people who are prepared to do that.' Such a sentiment would have been unintelligible. Anyone who really knew, supposed themselves to know, the truth, say a Catholic who believed in the truths preached to him by the Church, would have known that persons able to put the whole of themselves into the theory and practice of falsehood were simply dangerous persons, and that the more sincere they were, the more dangerous, the more mad.

No Christian knight would have supposed, when he fought against the Muslim, that he was expected to admire the purity and the sincerity with which the paynim believed in their absurd doctrines. No doubt if you were a decent person, and you killed a brave enemy, you were not obliged to spit upon his corpse. You took the line that it was a pity that so much courage (which was a universally admired quality), so much ability, so much devotion should have been expended on a cause so palpably absurd or dangerous. But you would not have said, 'It matters little what these people believe, what matters is the state of mind in which they believe it. What matters is that they did not sell out, that they were men of integrity. These are people I can respect. If they had come over to our side simply in order to save themselves, that would have been a very self-seeking, a very prudent, a very contemptible form of action.' This is the state of mind in which people must say, 'If I believe one thing, and you believe another, then it is important that we should fight each other. Perhaps it is good that you should kill me, or that I should kill you; perhaps, in a duel, it is best that we should kill each other; but the worst of all possible things is compromise, because that means we have both betrayed the ideal which is within us.'

Martyrdom, of course, was always admired, but martyrdom for the truth. Christians admired martyrs because they were witnesses to the truth. If they were witnesses to falsehood there was nothing admirable about them: perhaps something to be pitied, certainly nothing to be admired. By the 1820s you find an outlook in which the state of mind, the motive, is more important than the consequence, the intention is more important than the effect. Purity of heart, integrity, devotion, dedication – all these things which we ourselves admire without much difficulty, which have entered into the very texture of our normal moral attitudes, became more or less commonplace, first among minorities; then gradually they spread outwards.

Let me give an example of what I mean by this shift. Take Voltaire's play on Muhammad. Voltaire was not particularly interested in Muhammad, and the play was really intended, no doubt, as an attack upon the Church. Nevertheless Muhammad emerges as a superstitious, cruel and fanatical monster, who crushes all efforts at freedom, at justice, at reason, and is therefore to be denounced as an enemy of all that Voltaire held most important: toleration, justice, truth, civilisation. Then consider what, very much later, Carlyle has to say. Muhammad is described by Carlyle – who is a highly characteristic, if somewhat exaggerated, representative of the romantic movement – in a book called *On Heroes, Hero-Worship, and the Heroic in History*, in the course of which a great many heroes are enumerated and analysed. Muhammad is described as 'a fiery mass of Life cast up from the great bosom of Nature herself'. He is a man of blazing sincerity and power, and therefore to be admired; what he is compared to, what is not liked, is the eighteenth century, which is withered and useless, which to Carlyle, as he puts it, is a warped and second-rate century. Carlyle is not in the least interested in the truths of the Koran, he does not begin to suppose that the Koran contains anything which he, Carlyle, could be expected to believe. What he admires Muhammad for is that he is an elemental force, that he lives an intense life, that he has a great many followers with him; that something elemental occurred, a tremendous phenomenon, that there was a great and moving episode in the life of mankind, which Muhammad instantiates.

The importance of Muhammad is his character and not his beliefs. The question of whether what Muhammad believed was true or false would have appeared to Carlyle perfectly irrelevant. He says, in the course of the same essays, 'Dante's sublime Catholicism . . . has to be torn asunder by a Luther; Shakespeare's noble feudalism . . . has to end in a French Revolution.' Why do they have to do this? Because it does not matter whether Dante's sublime Catholicism is or is not true. The point is that it is a great movement, it has lasted its time, and now something equally powerful, equally earnest, equally sincere, equally deep, equally earth-shaking must take its place. The importance of the French Revolution is that it made a great dent upon the consciences of mankind; that the men who made the French Revolution were deeply in earnest, and not simply smiling hypocrites, as Carlyle thought Voltaire to be. This is an attitude which is, I will not say brand new, because it is too dangerous to say that, but at any rate sufficiently new to be worthy of attention, and whatever it was that caused it, occurred, it seems to me, somewhere between the years 1760 and 1830. It began in Germany, and grew apace.

Let us consider another example of the sort of thing I mean – the attitude towards tragedy. Previous generations assumed that tragedy was always due to some kind of error. Someone got something wrong, someone made a mistake. Either it was a moral error, or it was an intellectual error. It might have been avoidable, or it might have been unavoidable. For the Greeks, tragedy was error which the Gods sent upon you, which no man subject to them could perhaps have avoided; but, in principle, if these men had been omniscient, they would not have committed those grave errors which they did commit, and therefore would not have brought misfortunes upon themselves. If Oedipus had known that Laius was his father, he would not have murdered him. This is true even of the tragedies of Shakespeare, to a certain degree. If Othello had known that Desdemona was innocent, none of the denouement of that particular tragedy could have occurred. Therefore tragedy is founded upon the inevitable, or perhaps avoidable, lack of something in men – knowledge, skill, moral courage, ability to live, to do the right thing when you see it, or whatever it may be. Better men – morally stronger, intellectually more adept, above all omniscient persons, who perhaps also had enough power – could always avoid that which in fact is the substance of tragedy.

This is not so for the early nineteenth century, or even for the late eighteenth. If you read Schiller's tragedy *The Robbers*, to which I shall return again, you will find that Karl Moor, the hero-villain, is a man who avenges himself upon a detestable society by becoming a brigand and committing a number of atrocious murders. He is punished for it, in the end, but if you ask 'Who is to blame? Is it the side from which he comes? Are its values totally corrupt, or totally insane? Which of the two sides is right?' there is no answer to be obtained in that tragedy, and the very question would have appeared to Schiller shallow and blind.

Here there is a collision, perhaps an unavoidable collision, between sets of values which are incompatible. Previous generations supposed that all good things could be reconciled. This is true no longer. If you read Büchner's tragedy *The Death of Danton*, in

which Robespierre finally causes the deaths of Danton and Des-
moulins in the course of the Revolution, and you ask 'Was
Robespierre wrong to do this?', the answer is no; the tragedy is
such that Danton, although he was a sincere revolutionary who
committed certain errors, did not deserve to die, and yet Robespierre was perfectly right in putting him to death. There is a
collision here of what Hegel afterwards called 'good with good'. It
is due not to error, but to some kind of conflict of an unavoidable
kind, of loose elements wandering about the earth, of values which
cannot be reconciled. What matters is that people should dedicate
themselves to these values with all that is in them. If they do that,
they are suitable heroes for tragedy. If they do not do so, then they
are philistines, then they are members of the bourgeoisie, then they
are no good and not worth writing about.

The figure who dominates the nineteenth century as an image is
the tousled figure of Beethoven in his garret. Beethoven is a man
who does what is in him. He is poor, he is ignorant, he is boorish.
His manners are bad, he knows little, and he is perhaps not a very
interesting figure, apart from the inspiration which drives him
forward. But he has not sold out. He sits in his garret and he
creates. He creates in accordance with the light which is within
him, and that is all that a man should do; that is what makes a man
a hero. Even if he is not a genius like Beethoven, even if, like the
hero of Balzac's *Le Chef d'oeuvre inconnu*, 'The Unknown
Masterpiece', he is mad, and covers his canvas with paints, so that
in the end there is nothing intelligible at all, just a fearful confusion
of unintelligible and irrational paint – even then this figure is
worthy of more than pity, he is a man who has dedicated himself to
an ideal, who has thrown away the world, who represents the most
heroic, the most self-sacrificing, the most splendid qualities which a
human being can have. Gautier, in the famous preface to *Mademoiselle de Maupin* in 1835, defending the notion of art for art's sake,
says, addressing the critics in general, and the public too, 'No,
imbeciles! No! Fools and cretins that you are, a book will not
make a plate of soup; a novel is not a pair of boots; a sonnet is not a
syringe; a drama is not a railway ... no, two hundred thousand
times, no.' Gautier's point is that the old defence of art (quite apart
from the particular school of social utility which he is attacking –

Saint-Simon, the utilitarians and the socialists), the notion that the purpose of art is to give pleasure to a large number of persons, or even to a small number of carefully trained *cognoscenti*, is not valid. The purpose of art is to produce beauty, and if the artist alone perceives that his object is beautiful, that is a sufficient end in life.

Clearly something occurred to have shifted consciousness to this degree, away from the notion that there are universal truths, universal canons of art, that all human activities were meant to terminate in getting things right, and that the criteria of getting things right were public, were demonstrable, that all intelligent men by applying their intellects would discover them – away from that to a wholly different attitude towards life, and towards action. Something clearly occurred. When we ask what, we are told that there was a great turning towards emotionalism, that there was a sudden interest in the primitive and the remote – the remote in time, and the remote in place – that there was an outbreak of craving for the infinite. Something is said about 'emotion recollected in tranquillity'; something is said – but it is not clear what this has to do with any of the things which I have just mentioned – about Scott's novels, Schubert's songs, Delacroix, the rise of State-worship, and German propaganda in favour of economic self-sufficiency; also about superhuman qualities, admiration of wild genius, outlaws, heroes, aestheticism, self-destruction.

What have all these things in common? If we try to discover, a somewhat startling prospect greets our view. Let me offer some definitions of romanticism which I have culled from the writings of some of the most eminent persons who have written on the subject; these show that the subject is by no means easy.

Stendhal says that the romantic is the modern and interesting, classicism is the old and the dull. This is not perhaps quite as simple as it sounds: what he means is that romanticism is a matter of understanding the forces which move in your own life, as opposed to some escape towards something obsolete. However, what he actually says, in the book on Racine and Shakespeare, is what I have just enunciated. But his contemporary Goethe says that romanticism is disease, it is the weak, the sickly, the battle-cry of a school of wild poets and Catholic reactionaries; whereas classicism is strong, fresh, gay, sound, like Homer and the Song of the Niebelungs. Nietzsche says it is not a disease but a therapy, a cure for a disease. Sismondi, a Swiss critic of considerable imagination, though not perhaps altogether friendly to romanticism, in spite of being a friend of Madame de Staël, says that romanticism is a union of love, religion and chivalry. But Friedrich von Gentz, who was Metternich's chief agent at this time, and a precise contemporary of Sismondi, says that it is one of the heads of a three-headed Hydra, the other two heads being reform and revolution; it is in fact a left-wing menace, a menace to religion, to tradition and to the past which must be stamped out. The young French romantics, 'les jeunes France', echo this by saying 'Le romantisme, c'est la révolution.' *Révolution* against what? Apparently against everything.

Heine says romanticism is the passion-flower sprung from the blood of Christ, a re-awakening of the poetry of the sleepwalking Middle Ages, dreaming spires that look at you with the deep dolorous eyes of grinning spectres. Marxists would add that it was indeed an escape from the horrors of the Industrial Revolution, and Ruskin would agree, saying it was a contrast of the beautiful past with the frightful and the monotonous present; this is a modification of Heine's view, but not all that different from it. But Taine says that romanticism is a bourgeois revolt against the aristocracy after 1789; romanticism is the expression of the energy and force of the new *arrivistes* – the exact opposite. It is the expression of the pushing, vigorous powers of the new bourgeoisie against the old, decent, conservative values of society and history. It is the expression not of weakness, nor of despair, but of brutal optimism.

Friedrich Schlegel, the greatest harbinger, the greatest herald and prophet of romanticism that ever lived, says there is in man a terrible unsatisfied desire to soar into infinity, a feverish longing to break through the narrow bonds of individuality. Sentiments not altogether unlike this can be found in Coleridge and indeed in Shelley too. But Ferdinand Brunetière, towards the end of the century, says that it is literary egotism, it is stressing of individuality at the expense of a larger world, it is the opposite of self-transcendence, it is sheer self-assertion; and the Baron Seillière says yes, and egomania and primitivism; and Irving Babbitt echoes this.

Friedrich Schlegel's brother August Wilhelm Schlegel and Madame de Staël agreed that romanticism comes from the Romance nations, or at least the Romance languages, that it really comes from a modification of the verses of the Provençal troubadours; but Renan says it is Celtic. Gaston Paris says it is Breton; Seillière says it comes from a mixture of Plato and pseudo-Dionysius the Areopagite. Joseph Nadler, a learned German critic, says that romanticism is really the homesickness of those Germans who lived between the Elbe and the Niemen – their homesickness for the old Central Germany from which they once came, the daydreams of exiles and colonists. Eichendorff says it is Protestant nostalgia for the Catholic Church. But Chateaubriand, who did not live between the Elbe and the Niemen, and therefore did not experience these emotions, says it is the secret and inexpressible delight of a soul playing with itself: 'I speak everlastingly of myself.' Joseph Aynard says it is the will to love something, an attitude or an emotion towards others, and not towards oneself, the very opposite of the will to power. Middleton Murry says Shakespeare was essentially a romantic writer, and adds that all great writers since Rousseau have been romantic. But the eminent Marxist critic Georg Lukács says no great writers are romantic, least of all Scott, Hugo and Stendhal.

If we consider these quotations from men who after all deserve to be read, who are in other respects profound and brilliant writers on many subjects, it is clear that there is some difficulty in discovering the common element in all these generalisations. That is why Northrop Frye was so very wise to warn against it. All these competing definitions have never, so far as I know, really been the subject of a protest by anyone; they have never incurred that degree of critical wrath which might have been unleashed against anyone who had really produced definitions or generalisations which were universally regarded as absurd and irrelevant.

The next step is to see what characteristics have been called romantic by writers on this subject, by critics. A very peculiar result emerges. There is such variety among the examples I have accumulated that the difficulty of the subject which I was unwise enough to choose seems even more extreme.

Romanticism is the primitive, the untutored, it is youth, the exuberant sense of life of the natural man, but it is also pallor, fever, disease, decadence, the *maladie du siècle*, La Belle Dame Sans Merci, the Dance of Death, indeed Death itself. It is Shelley's dome of many-coloured glass, and it is also his white radiance of eternity. It is the confused teeming fullness and richness of life, *Fülle des Lebens*, inexhaustible multiplicity, turbulence, violence, conflict, chaos, but also it is peace, oneness with the great 'I Am', harmony with the natural order, the music of the spheres, dissolution in the eternal all-containing spirit. It is the strange, the exotic, the grotesque, the mysterious, the supernatural, ruins, moonlight, enchanted castles, hunting horns, elves, giants, griffins, falling water, the old mill on the Floss, darkness and the powers of darkness, phantoms, vampires, nameless terror, the irrational, the unutterable. Also it is the familiar, the sense of one's unique tradition, joy in the smiling aspect of everyday nature, and the accustomed sights and sounds of contented, simple, rural folk – the sane and happy wisdom of rosy-cheeked sons of the soil. It is the ancient, the historic, it is Gothic cathedrals, mists of antiquity, ancient roots and the old order with its unanalysable qualities, its profound but inexpressible loyalties, the impalpable, the imponderable. Also it is the pursuit of novelty, revolutionary change, concern with the fleeting present, desire to live in the moment, rejection of knowledge, past and future, the pastoral idyll of happy innocence, joy in the passing instant, a sense of timelessness. It is nostalgia, it is reverie, it is intoxicating dreams, it is sweet melancholy and bitter melancholy, solitude, the sufferings of exile, the sense of alienation, roaming in remote places, especially the East, and in remote times, especially the Middle Ages. But also it is happy co-operation in a common creative effort, the sense of forming part of a Church, a class, a party, a tradition, a great and all-containing symmetrical hierarchy, knights and retainers, the ranks of the Church, organic social ties, mystic unity, one faith, one land, one blood, 'la terre et les morts', as Barrès said, the great society of the dead and the living and the yet unborn. It is the Toryism of Scott and Southey and Wordsworth, and it is the radicalism of Shelley, Büchner and Stendhal. It is Chateaubriand's aesthetic medievalism, and it is Michelet's loathing of the Middle Ages. It is Carlyle's worship of authority, and Hugo's hatred of authority. It is extreme nature mysticism, and extreme anti-naturalist aestheticism. It is energy, force, will, life, *étalage du moi*; it is also self-torture, self-annihilation, suicide. It is the primitive, the unsophisticated, the bosom of nature, green fields, cow-bells, murmuring brooks, the infinite blue sky. No less, however, it is also dandyism, the desire to dress up, red waistcoats, green wigs, blue hair, which the followers of people like Gérard de Nerval wore in Paris at a certain period. It is the lobster which Nerval led about on a string in the streets of Paris. It is wild exhibitionism, eccentricity, it is the battle of Ernani, it is *ennui*, it is *taedium vitae*, it is the death of Sardanopolis, whether painted by Delacroix, or written about by Berlioz or Byron. It is the convulsion of great empires, wars, slaughter and the crashing of worlds. It is the romantic hero – the rebel, *l'homme fatal*, the damned soul, the Corsairs, Manfreds, Giaours, Laras, Cains, all the population of Byron's heroic poems. It is Melmoth, it is Jean Sbogar, all the outcasts and Ishmaels as well as the golden-hearted courtesans and the noble-hearted convicts of nineteenth-century fiction. It is drinking out of the human skull, it is Berlioz who said he wanted to climb Vesuvius in order to commune with a kindred soul. It is Satanic revels, cynical irony, diabolical laughter, black heroes, but also Blake's vision of God and his angels, the great Christian society, the eternal order, and 'the starry heavens which can scarce express the infinite and eternal of the Christian soul'. It is, in short, unity and multiplicity. It is fidelity to the particular, in the paintings of nature for example, and also mysterious tantalising vagueness of outline. It is beauty and ugliness. It is art for art's sake, and art as an instrument of social salvation. It is strength and weakness, individualism and collectivism, purity and corruption, revolution and reaction, peace and war, love of life and love of death.

It is perhaps not very surprising that, faced with this, A. O. Lovejoy, who is certainly the most scrupulous and one of the most illuminating scholars who ever dealt with the history of the ideas of the last two centuries, approached a condition nearing despair. He unravelled as many strands of romantic thought as he was able to, and not only found that some of them contradict the others, which is patently true, and that some are totally irrelevant to the others, but he went further. He took two specimens of what nobody would deny to be romanticism, for example, primitivism and eccentricity – dandyism – and asked what they had in common. Primitivism, which began in English verse and to some extent in English prose at the beginning of the eighteenth century, celebrates the noble savage, the simple life, the irregular patterns of spontaneous action, as against the corrupt sophistication and Alexandrine verse of a highly sophisticated society. It is an attempt to demonstrate that there is a natural law which can be discovered best in the untutored heart of the uncorrupted native, or the uncorrupted child. What, asks Lovejoy quite intelligibly, has this in common with red waistcoats, blue hair, green wigs, absinthe, death, suicide and the general eccentricity of the followers of Nerval and Gautier? He concludes by saying that he really does not see what there is in common, and one can sympathise with him. One might say, perhaps, that there is an air of revolt in both, that both have revolted against some kind of civilisation, one in order to go to some Robinson Crusoe island, there to commune with nature and live among uncorrupted simple people, and the other in pursuit of some kind of violent aestheticism and dandyism. But mere revolt, mere denunciation of corruption cannot be romantic. We do not regard the Hebrew prophets or Savonarola or even Methodist preachers as particularly romantic. This is too wide of the mark. One does therefore have a certain sympathy with Lovejoy's despair.

Let me quote a passage which Lovejoy's disciple George Boas wrote apropos of this:

> [A]fter the discrimination of the romanticisms made by Lovejoy, there ought to be no further discussion of what romanticism *really* was. There happen to have been a variety of aesthetic doctrines, some of which were logically related to others and some of which were not, all called by the same name. But that fact does not imply they all had a common essence, any more than the fact that hundreds of people are called John Smith means that they are all of the same parentage. This is perhaps the most common and misleading error arising from the confusion of ideas and words. One could speak for hours about it alone and perhaps should.

I should like to relieve your fears immediately by saying that I do not propose to do this. But at the same time I think that both Lovejoy and Boas, eminent scholars though they are, and great though their contribution has been towards illumination of thought, are in this instance mistaken. There *was* a romantic movement; it did have something which was central to it; it did create a great revolution in consciousness; and it is important to discover what this is.

One can of course give up the whole game. One can say, like Valéry, that words like *romanticism* and *classicism*, words like *humanism* and *naturalism*, are not names with which one can operate at all. 'One cannot get drunk, one cannot quench one's thirst, with labels on bottles.' There is much to be said for this point of view. At the same time, unless we do use some generalisations it is impossible to trace the course of human history. Therefore, difficult as it may be, it is important to find out what it was that caused this enormous revolution in human consciousness which occurred in those centuries. There are people who, faced with this plethora of evidence which I have attempted to collect, may feel some sympathy for the late Sir Arthur Quiller-Couch, who said with typical British breeziness, 'The whole pother about [the difference between classicism and romanticism] amounts to nothing that need trouble a healthy man.'

I cannot deny that I do not share this point of view. It appears to me to be excessively defeatist. Therefore I shall do my best to explain what in my view the romantic movement fundamentally came to. The only sane and sensible way of approaching it, at least the only way that I have ever found to be at all helpful, is by slow and patient historical method; by looking at the beginning of the eighteenth century and considering what the situation was then, and then considering what the factors were which undermined it, one by one, and what the particular combination or confluence of factors was which, by the later part of the century, caused what appears to me to be the greatest transformation of Western consciousness, certainly in our time.

2

THE FIRST ATTACK ON ENLIGHTENMENT

THE ENLIGHTENMENT of the late seventeenth and early eighteenth centuries needs some definition. There are three propositions, if we may boil it down to that, which are, as it were, the three legs upon which the whole Western tradition rested. They are not confined to the Enlightenment, although the Enlightenment offered a particular version of them, transformed them in a particular manner. The three principles are roughly these. First, that all genuine questions can be answered, that if a question cannot be answered it is not a question. We may not know what the answer is, but someone else will. We may be too weak, or too stupid, or too ignorant, to be able to discover the answer for ourselves. In that case the answer may perhaps be known to persons wiser than us – to experts, an élite of some sort. We may be sinful creatures, and therefore incapable of ever arriving at the truth by ourselves. In that case, we shall not know it in this world, but perhaps in the next. Or perhaps it was known in some golden age before the Fall and the Flood had rendered us as weak and as sinful as we are. Or perhaps the golden age is not in the past, but in the future, and we shall discover the truth then. If not here, there. If not now, at some other time. But in principle the answer must be known, if not to men, then at any rate to an omniscient being, to God. If the answer is not knowable at all, if the answer is in some way in principle shrouded from us, then there must be something wrong with the question. This is a proposition which is common both to Christians and to scholastics, to the Enlightenment and to the positivist tradition of the twentieth century. It is, in fact, the backbone of the main Western tradition, and it is this that romanticism cracked.

The second proposition is that all these answers are knowable, that they can be discovered by means which can be learnt and taught to other persons; that there are techniques by which it is possible to learn and to teach ways of discovering what the world consists of, what part we occupy in it, what our relation is to people, what our relation is to things, what true values are, and the answer to every other serious and answerable question.

The third proposition is that all the answers must be compatible with one another, because, if they are not compatible, then chaos will result. It is clear that the true answer to one question cannot be incompatible with the true answer to another question. It is a logical truth that one true proposition cannot contradict another. If all answers to all questions are to be put in the form of propositions, and if all true propositions are in principle discoverable, then it must follow that there is a description of an ideal universe – a Utopia, if you like – which is simply that which is described by all true answers to all serious questions. This Utopia, although we may not be able to attain to it, is at any rate that ideal in terms of which we can measure off our own present imperfections.

Those are the general presuppositions of the rationalist Western tradition, whether Christian or pagan, whether theist or atheist. The particular twist which the Enlightenment gave to this tradition was to say that the answers were not to be obtained in many of the hitherto traditional ways – I need not dwell on that, for it will be familiar. The answer is not to be obtained by revelation, for different men's revelations appear to contradict each other. It is not to be obtained by tradition, because tradition can be shown to be often misleading and false. It is not to be obtained by dogma, it is not to be obtained by the individual self-inspection of men of a privileged type, because too many impostors have usurped this role – and so forth. There is only one way of discovering these answers, and that is by the correct use of reason, deductively as in the mathematical sciences, inductively as in the sciences of nature. That is the only way in which answers in general – true answers to serious questions – may be obtained. There is no reason why such answers, which after all have produced triumphant results in the worlds of physics and chemistry, should not equally apply to the much more troubled fields of politics, ethics and aesthetics.

The general pattern, I wish to stress, of this notion is that life, or nature,[1] is a jigsaw puzzle. We lie among the disjected fragments of this puzzle. There must be some means of putting these pieces together. The all-wise man, the omniscient being, whether God or an omniscient earthly creature – whichever way you like to conceive it – is in principle capable of fitting all the various pieces together into one coherent pattern. Anyone who does this will know what the world is like: what things are, what they have been, what they will be, what the laws are that govern them, what man is, what the relation of man is to things, and therefore what man needs, what he desires, and also how to obtain it. All questions, whether of a factual nature or of what we call a normative nature – questions such as 'What should I do?' or 'What ought I to do?' or 'What would it be right or appropriate for me to do?' – all these questions are answerable by someone who is capable of fitting together the pieces of the jigsaw puzzle. It is like a hunt for some kind of concealed treasure. The only difficulty is to find the path to the treasure. Upon this, of course, theorists have differed. But in the eighteenth century there was a fairly wide consensus that what Newton had achieved in the region of physics could surely also be applied to the regions of ethics and of politics.

The regions of ethics and politics presented a rare disorder. It was perfectly clear, then as now, that people did not know what the answers to these questions were. How should one live? Were republics preferable to monarchies? Was it right to seek pleasure, or to do one's duty, or could these alternatives be reconciled? Was it right to be ascetic, or was it right to be a voluptuary? Was it proper to obey élites of specialists who knew the truth, or was it the case that every man had the right to his own particular opinion as to what he should do? Was the majority opinion to be taken as of necessity the correct answer to political life? Was the good something which was intuited as an external property, as something that was out there, eternal, objective, true for all men in all

---

[1] When seventeenth- and eighteenth-century authors say 'nature', we can translate that into 'life' perfectly easily. The word 'nature' was as much a commonplace in the eighteenth century as the word 'creative' is now, and had about as precise a meaning.

circumstances everywhere, or was the good only something which a particular person in a particular situation happened to like or happened to be inclined towards?

These questions were, then as now, of a puzzling nature. It was quite natural that people should point to Newton, who had found physics in a very similar state, with a great many criss-crossing hypotheses, founded upon a great deal of classical and scholastic error. With a very few masterly strokes he had managed to reduce this enormous chaos to comparative order. From a very few clear physico-mathematical propositions he was able to deduce the position and the velocity of every particle in the universe; or if not to deduce them, to place weapons in people's hands with which they could, if they applied themselves, deduce them; weapons which any intelligent man could in principle use for himself. Surely, if this kind of order could be instituted in the world of physics, the same methods would produce equally splendid and lasting results in the worlds of morals, politics, aesthetics, and in the rest of the chaotic world of human opinion, where people appeared to struggle with each other, and murder each other and destroy each other, and humiliate each other, in the name of incompatible principles. This appeared to be a perfectly reasonable hope, and it appeared to be a very worthy human ideal. At any rate this is certainly the ideal of the Enlightenment.

The Enlightenment was certainly not, as is sometimes maintained, a kind of uniform movement of which all the members believed approximately the same things. For example, opinions about human nature differed very widely. Fontenelle and Saint-Évremond, Voltaire and La Mettrie thought that man was hopelessly jealous, envious, wicked, corrupt and weak; and therefore he needed the most strenuous possible discipline just to keep his head above water. He needed a rigid discipline to enable him to cope with life at all. Others did not take quite so black a view, and thought that man was essentially a malleable substance, clay which any competent educator, any enlightened legislator, could mould into perfectly proper and rational shape. There were, of course, a few persons, such as Rousseau, who thought that man was naturally neither neutral nor wicked, but good, and had been ruined only by institutions of his own making. If these institutions could be altered or reformed in a very drastic way, man's natural goodness would burst forth, and the reign of love could be once again created upon the earth.

Again, some eminent doctrinaires of the Enlightenment believed in the immortality of the soul. Others believed that the notion of a soul was a hollow superstition, that there was no such entity. Some believed in the élite, in the necessity of government by the wise; that the mob would never learn; that there was an inequality of gifts which was permanent among mankind, and unless men could somehow be trained or induced to obey those who knew, the élite of experts – as they do in the case of techniques which clearly need them, such as navigation or economics – life on earth would continue to be a jungle. Others believed that in matters of ethics and politics every man was his own expert; that while not everyone could be a good mathematician, all men by inspecting their own hearts could know the difference between good and evil, right and wrong; the reason they did not know it now was only that they had been misled by knaves or fools in the past, by self-interested rulers, wicked soldiers, corrupt priests and other enemies of man. If these persons could be eliminated or liquidated in some way, then clear answers could be discovered by every man, graven in eternal letters upon his own heart, as Rousseau preached.

There were other disagreements as well, into which I need not go. But what is common to all these thinkers is the view that virtue consists ultimately in knowledge; that if we know what we are, and we know what we need, and we know where to obtain it, and we obtain it by the best means in our possession, then we can live happy, virtuous, just, free and contented lives; that all virtues are compatible with one another; that it is impossible for it to be the case that the answer to the question 'Should one seek justice?' is 'Yes', and the answer to the question 'Should one seek mercy?' is 'Yes', and that these two answers should somehow prove incompatible. Equality, liberty, fraternity must be compatible with one another. So must mercy and justice. If a man were to say that the truth could make someone miserable, this must somehow be demonstrated to be false. If it could be shown that in some way total liberty was incompatible with total equality, there must be some misunderstanding in the argument – and so on. This was a belief which all these men held. Above all they held that these general propositions were obtainable by the dependable methods used by natural scientists in the establishing of the great triumph of the eighteenth century – namely the natural sciences themselves.

Before I turn to the particular form taken by the attack upon the Enlightenment, let me explain that of course this outlook penetrates as much into the realm of the arts as it does into that of the sciences and that of ethics. For example, the dominant aesthetic theory of the early eighteenth century was that man should hold up a mirror to nature. Put like that, it seems rather crude and misleading; in fact, a falsehood. To hold up a mirror to nature is merely to copy what is already there. This is not what these theorists meant by this phrase. By nature they meant life, and by life they meant not what one saw, but that towards which they supposed life to strive, certain ideal forms towards which all life was tending. No doubt it was a clever thing on the part of the painter Zeuxis in Athens to paint grapes so realistically that birds came to peck at them. It was very skilful on the part of Raphael to paint gold pieces so accurately that the innkeeper thought them to be genuine and let him go without paying his account. But these were not the highest flights of human artistic genius. The highest artistic genius consisted in somehow visualising that inner objective ideal towards which nature and man tended, and somehow embodying this in a noble painting. That is, there is some kind of universal pattern, and this the artist is able to incorporate in images, as the philosopher or the scientist is capable of incorporating it in propositions.

Let me quote a very typical statement by Fontenelle, the most representative of all the figures of the Enlightenment, who led a very careful and very rational life, which enabled him to live to the age of a hundred. He said: 'A work of politics, of morality, of criticism, perhaps even of literature, will be finer, all things considered, if made by the hands of a geometer.' That is because geometers are persons who understand the rational interrelationships of things. Anybody who understands the pattern which nature follows – because nature is surely a rational entity, otherwise man would not be able to conceive it or understand it at all (that was the argument) – is surely able to elicit from the apparent chaos and confusion of nature those eternal principles, those necessary connections, which bind together the eternal and objective elements out of which the world is composed. René Rapin in the seventeenth century said that Aristotle's poetics is only 'nature reduced to method, good sense reduced to principle'; and Pope repeated that in famous lines, saying:

> Those RULES of old *discover'd* not *devis'd*,
> Are *Nature* still, but *Nature Methodiz'd*.

That, roughly speaking, is the official doctrine of the eighteenth century, namely that you discover the method in nature herself. Reynolds, probably the most representative eighteenth-century aesthetic theorist, certainly in England, said that the painter corrects nature by herself, her imperfect state by her more perfect; he perceives an abstract idea of forms more perfect than any real original. This is the famous ideal beauty by which, he says, Phidias acquired his immortal fame. Therefore we must understand what it is that the ideal consists of.

The notion is this. There are certain persons who are more eminent than others. Alexander the Great is a more splendid figure than a lame or blind beggar, and therefore deserves more of the artist than the beggar, who is a mere accident of nature. Nature tends towards perfection. We know what perfection is by some inner sense, which tells us what is the norm and what is abnormal, what is the ideal and what is the deviation from this ideal. Therefore, says Reynolds with great firmness, if Alexander had happened to be of low stature, we should not render him so. Bernini should never have let David bite his lower lip, because that is a mean expression, inappropriate to royal rank. If St Paul was of mean appearance, as we are told, Raphael was right not so to draw him. Perrault, writing towards the end of the seventeenth century, says it is a great pity that Homer allows his heroes to be too familiar with swineherds. He does not, I suppose, wish to deny that perhaps Homer's heroes, or persons from whom he drew his originals, might have been as familiar with swineherds as they are represented as being, but if so, they should not have been. The business of the painter is not simply realistically to reproduce what is there – that is what the Dutch too often do, and this merely populates the world with a number of copies of entities which originally had no need to be there.

The purpose of painting is to convey to the questing intellect or the questing soul what it is that nature seeks after. Nature seeks after beauty and perfection. All these people believed that. Nature may not have attained to these ideals; in particular, man has conspicuously not attained to them. But by inspecting nature we observe the general lines upon which she proceeds. We see what it is that she strives to produce. We know the difference between a stunted oak and a fully-grown oak; we know, when we call it stunted, that it is an oak which has failed to become that which it was intended by itself, or by nature, to be. In the same way there are objective ideals of beauty, of grandeur, of magnificence, of wisdom, which it is the business of writers, philosophers, preachers, painters, sculptors – composers, too – in some way to convey to us. That is the general notion.

Johann Joachim Winckelmann, the most original of all the aesthetic theorists of the eighteenth century, who introduced this passionate nostalgic taste for classical art, speaks about 'noble simplicity' and 'calm grandeur'. Why noble simplicity? Why calm grandeur? He does not suppose any more than anyone else that all the ancients were nobly simple, or calmly grand, but he does think that this is the ideal conception of what man should be. He does think that to be a Roman senator, or to be a Greek orator – or whatever it is that he regarded as the perfection of man, what all the Germans in his time tended to think of as the most perfect man – was to be a person who tended towards this noblest of human ideals; and that the sculptors who immortalised these particular traits hold up before us the ideal of what man can be, and in this way not only inspire us to imitate these ideals but reveal to us the inner purposes of nature, reveal to us reality. Reality, life, nature, the ideal – these things are identical for these thinkers.

Just as mathematics deals in perfect circles, so the sculptor and the painter must deal in ideal forms. This is the rationalist notion of most eighteenth-century aesthetics. That is why there is a comparative neglect of history. Although it is true that Voltaire was the first person who began no longer to write the history of individual kings and conquerors, captains and adventurers, but to take an interest in people's morals, their clothes, their habits, their judicial institutions; although some interest in the general history of people's manners, as well as individual conquests and treaties, had got going in the eighteenth century, nevertheless there is no doubt that, when Bolingbroke said that history was nothing but 'philosophy teaching by examples', he was voicing a very common view.

Voltaire's interest in history was to show how men were much the same in most ages, and how the same causes produce the same effects. The purpose of that was to show what we were like sociologically: what kind of ends men sought after, what kind of means did not bring them about, what kind of means did bring them about – and in this way to create some kind of science of how to live well. The same is true of Hume, who also spoke in much the same way. He said that most men in most circumstances, obeying the same causes, behave in roughly the same fashion. The purpose of history is not simply curiosity about what happened in the past, or desire to revive it, simply because we feel passionately interested in what our ancestors were like, or because we wish in some way to connect the past with ourselves, to see what it was that we grew out of. That was not the principal spring of these men's interest. Their main aim was simply the accumulation of data upon which general propositions could be constructed, telling one what to do, how to live, what to be. That is the most unhistorical possible attitude that can be taken towards history, and it is the fairly characteristic attitude of the eighteenth century, including great historians who, despite themselves, wrote great history, such as Gibbon, whose ideals were a great deal inferior to his actual performance.

These being the general notions of the Enlightenment, it is clear that, in the case of the arts, they would lead to the formal, the noble, the symmetrical, the proportional, the judicious. There were, of course, exceptions to this. I do not say that everybody believed exactly the same thing: this is very uncommon in any age. Even in classical France there were all kinds of aberrations: quietists and convulsionists – persons of hysterical or ecstatic temperament. There were people like Vauvenargues, who complained bitterly about the appalling emptiness of life. There was

Madame de la Popelinière, who said she wished to throw herself out of the window because she felt that life had no meaning and no purpose. But these were, comparatively, a minority. Broadly speaking, it could be said that it was Voltaire and his friends, people like Helvétius, people like Fontenelle, who represented the major position of the age, and this was that we were progressing, we were discovering, we were destroying ancient prejudice, superstition, ignorance and cruelty, and we were well on the way towards establishing some kind of science which would make people happy, free, virtuous and just. It was this that was attacked by the persons I shall turn to next.

Certain cracks in this rather smug and smooth wall had already been made by the Enlightenment itself. For example, Montesquieu, a fairly typical representative of the Enlightenment, had suggested that men were not the same everywhere, and this proposition, which had already been uttered by a good many Greek Sophists, but had been forgotten in the meantime, did make a sort of dent in the general picture, though not a very deep one. Montesquieu's point was that if you were a Persian and brought up in Persian conditions, you might not want what you would want if you were a Parisian and brought up in Paris; that men were not made happy by the same things, that the attempt to foist upon the Chinese things that delighted the French, or upon the French things that delighted the Chinese, would cause misery in both cases; and that therefore one had to be very careful, in altering laws, in reforming and in generally looking after people, if one was a statesman, or a politician, or even in personal relations, in friendship, in family life, to consider what people's actual needs are, what is the relevant process of growth, what are the conditions in which a specific body of persons grew up. He attached enormous importance to soil, climate and political institutions. Others attached importance to other factors, but whichever way you look at it, the basic notion was that of a general relativism, that what did for people in Birmingham would not do for people in Bukhara.

In a sense, of course, this did contradict the proposition that there were certain objective, uniform, eternal, fixed entities, for example certain forms of pleasure which pleased everyone everywhere; that there were certain true propositions which all men at all times could have discovered for themselves, but failed to do so only because they were too stupid or placed in unfortunate circumstances; that there was a unique form of life which, once it is introduced into the universe, could be fixed as eternal, would not need to be altered, because it was perfect, because it satisfied the permanent interests and desires of men. Views like Montesquieu's did contradict that, but not very sharply. All Montesquieu said was that, although all men in fact sought the same things, namely happiness, contentment, harmony, justice, liberty – none of this he denied – different circumstances made different means of attaining these things necessary. This was a very sensible remark, and did not in principle contradict the foundations of the Enlightenment.

Montesquieu did make an observation which shocked people. He said that when Montezuma said to Cortés that the Christian religion was all very well for Spain, but that the Aztec religion might be best for his people, what he said was not absurd. This, of course, did shock both parties. It shocked the Roman Church, and it shocked the left wing. It shocked the Roman Church for obvious reasons. It shocked the left wing too because they too knew that since what the Catholic Church said was false, the opposite was true; since what the Aztec religion said was false, the opposite was true. Therefore the notion that propositions which might not appear true to us might yet do for some other culture, that one ought to estimate the value of religious truths not in accordance with some objective standard but by some much more flexible or pragmatic means, namely by asking whether it made the people who believed them happy, suited their way of life, developed certain ideals among them, fitted into the general texture of their life and experience – that appeared to both sides, both the Roman Church and the atheistical materialists, to be a betrayal. Nevertheless, this is the kind of criticism which Montesquieu made, and, as I say, it modified the picture somewhat. It did modify the proposition that there were eternal truths, eternal institutions, eternal values, suitable for everyone, everywhere. You had to be more flexible. You had to say: Well, not eternal perhaps, not everywhere; most people, in most places, with due adjustment made for time and place. But if you did that you could still preserve the foundations of the views of the Enlightenment.

A somewhat deeper breach was made by Hume. Carl Becker, in his very intelligent, interesting, amusing and remarkable book, *The Heavenly City of the Eighteenth-Century Philosophers*, argues that Hume blew up the entire Enlightenment position by showing that the necessities in which these philosophers believed, the network of rigorous logical relationships of which the universe consisted and which reason could grasp and live by, did not really exist; and that therefore Hume undermined the general notion of a kind of seamless garment or harmony of necessary connections.

I do not agree with Becker about this, though I shall not go into this in detail. Hume's chief service in his attack on the Enlightenment – and he certainly did not appear to himself to be mounting such an attack – consisted in doubting two propositions. In the first place he doubted whether the causal relationship was something which we directly perceived, or indeed knew to exist at all. He said that, so far from things being necessitated by other things, they just followed along in a regular manner, without being necessitated. Instead of saying causes must produce effects, or this event must produce that event, or this situation cannot help arising from that situation, all you needed to say was: Usually this situation follows that situation; normally, this thing is to be found before or at the same time as or after that thing – which for practical purposes did not make a great deal of difference.

The second proposition doubted by Hume is more important for our purposes. When he asked himself how he knew that there was an external world at all, he said he could not deduce it logically: there was no way of demonstrating that tables existed. There was no way of demonstrating that at this moment I am eating an egg, or drinking a glass of water. I can demonstrate things in geometry. I can demonstrate things in arithmetic. I can demonstrate things in logic. I might, I suppose, be able to demonstrate things in heraldry or chess, or in other sciences which follow from artificial rules, conventionally established. But I cannot prove with mathematical certainty that anything exists. All I can say is that, if I ignore a thing, I shall rue it. If I suppose that there is no table in front of me, and walk into it, I shall probably suffer discomfort. But demonstrate it in the sense in which I can demonstrate mathematical propositions, demonstrate it in the sense in which I can demonstrate a proposition in logic, where the opposite is not merely false but meaningless, that I cannot do. Therefore I must accept the world as a matter of belief, on trust. Belief is not the same as deductive certainty. Indeed, deduction does not apply to matters of fact at all.

Without going into the vast consequences which this had in the general history of logic and philosophy, we can see that it clearly did weaken the general position according to which the universe was a rational whole, each part of which was as it was necessarily – because it was necessitated by the other parts of it – and the whole thing was made beautiful and rational by the fact that none of the things in it could be otherwise than as they were. The old belief was that whatever was true was necessarily true, that things could not be otherwise than as they were, and that is why, said Spinoza (and people who thought like him), when I understand that things are inevitable, I accept them much more willingly. No man wants to believe that two plus two equals five; anyone who says, 'Two plus two has always equalled four, but this is a very suffocating truth – could it not be the case occasionally that two plus two would be four-and-a-half or seventeen?', anyone who wanted to break out of the hideous prison of the multiplication table, would be regarded as not quite sane. The proposition that two plus two equals four, or the proposition that if A is larger than B, and B is larger than C, then A is larger than C – these kinds of propositions are propositions which we accept as being part of the general rational process of thought, part of what we mean by sanity, by rationality. If all facts in the universe could be reduced to this level, then we should no longer kick against them. That is the great rationalist presupposition. If all the things which at present you hate and fear could be so represented as to flow by necessary logical chains from everything else that there was, you would accept them as being not only inevitable but reasonable, and therefore delightful, as much as 'Two plus two equals four' or any other logical truth upon which you found your life, upon which your thought rests. That ideal of rationalism Hume certainly broke.

In spite of the fact that Montesquieu and Hume did make these faint dents in the outlook of the Enlightenment – one by showing that not everything was everywhere the same, the other by saying that there were no necessities, only probabilities – the difference they made was not very large. Hume certainly thought that the universe would continue to proceed much as it had done before. He certainly thought that there were rational and irrational courses of action, that men could be made happy by rational means. He believed in science, he believed in reason, he believed in cool judgement, he believed in all the well-known propositions of the eighteenth century. He believed in art exactly as Reynolds believed in it, exactly as Dr Johnson believed in it. The logical implications of his ideas did not really become evident until the late nineteenth and twentieth centuries. The attack which I wish to discuss came from a very different quarter – from the Germans.

The truth about the Germans in the seventeenth and eighteenth centuries is that they constitute a somewhat backward province. They do not wish to think of themselves in this light, but it remains true to describe them in these terms. In the sixteenth century the Germans were as progressive and as dynamic and as generous in their contribution to European culture as anyone else. Certainly Dürer was as great a painter as any European painter of his time. Certainly Luther was as great a religious figure as anyone in European history. But if you look at Germany in the seventeenth century, and in the early eighteenth century, then for whatever reason, with the exception of the one great figure of Leibniz, who is certainly a philosopher of world scale, it is very difficult to find anyone among the Germans of that time who affected the thought or even the art of the world in any significant fashion, particularly towards the end of the seventeenth century.

What the reason is for this is rather difficult to say. Not being a competent historian, I do not wish to volunteer too much. But for some reason or other the Germans failed to achieve centralised statehood in the way that England and France and even Holland achieved it. The Germans were governed in the eighteenth century, and indeed in the seventeenth, by three hundred princes and twelve hundred sub-princes. The Emperor had interests in Italy and elsewhere, which prevented him from paying due attention, perhaps, to his German lands; and above all there was the violent dislocation of the Thirty Years War, in the course of which foreign troops, including those of France, destroyed and killed a very large section of the German population and crushed what might have been a cultural development in seas of blood. This was a misfortune of an unexampled kind in European history. Such a number of persons had never been killed for any reason before, since the days of Genghis Khan, and the misfortune to Germany was crushing. It crushed her spirit to a very high degree, with the result that German culture became provincialised, became disrupted into these tiny stuffy provincial courts. There was no Paris, there was no centre, there was no life, there was no pride, there was no sense of growth, dynamism and power. German culture drifted either into extreme scholastic pedantry of a Lutheran kind – minute but rather dry scholarship – or else into a revolt against this scholarship in the direction of the inner life of the human soul. This was no doubt stimulated by Lutheranism as such, but particularly by the fact that there was a kind of huge national inferiority complex, which began at that period, vis-à-vis the great progressive Western States, particularly vis-à-vis the French, this brilliant glittering State which had managed to crush and humiliate them, this great country which dominated the sciences and the arts, and all the provinces of human life, with a kind of arrogance and success unexampled hitherto. This did plant in Germany a permanent sense of sadness and humiliation which may be discovered in the rather doleful German ballad literature and popular literature of the end of the seventeenth century, and even in the arts in which the Germans excelled – even in music, which tends to be domestic, religious, passionate, inward, and above all different from the glittering court art and splendid secular achievements of composers like Rameau and Couperin. There is no doubt that if you compare composers like Bach and his contemporaries, and Telemann, with French composers of that period, then although Bach's genius is incomparably greater, the whole atmosphere and tone of his music is much more, I will not say provincial, but confined to the particular inner religious life of the city of Leipzig (or wherever he happened to live), and was not intended to be an offering before the glittering courts of Europe, or for the general admiration of mankind, in the way in which the paintings and the musical

35

compositions of the English, the Dutch, the French and the other leading nations of the world were obviously intended.[1]

Against this background the pietist movement, which really is the root of romanticism, became deeply embedded in Germany. Pietism was a branch of Lutheranism, and consisted in careful study of the Bible and profound respect for the personal relationship of man to God. There was therefore an emphasis upon spiritual life, contempt for learning, contempt for ritual and for form, contempt for pomp and ceremony, and a tremendous stress upon the individual relationship of the individual suffering human soul with her maker. Spener, Francke, Zinzendorf, Arnold – all these founders of the pietist movement managed to bring comfort and salvation to a large collection of socially crushed and politically

---

[1] In October 1967 Berlin received a letter from I. Berz contesting these remarks on Bach. In his reply, dated 30 October 1967, Berlin wrote: 'Of course what I said was much too sweeping, as happens in lectures of this kind, and I should not say it in print [. . .] Bach, as you rightly say, composed court music in Weimar, Cöthen and so on, and was delighted when the King invited him to Berlin and paid great respect to the Royal theme, on which he then wrote those famous variations [. . .] Nor are even the Goldberg variations to be regarded as a piece of *innig*, soul-searching music. All this is true.

'The point I wished to make was that the bulk of Bach's compositions were composed in a pietistic atmosphere – that there was a tradition of religious inwardness by which the Germans insulated themselves to a large degree from the worldly superficialities, brilliance, search for world fame and general glitter of France and even Italy; that Bach himself never behaved as if he supposed himself to be a great and dominant figure in the world of music of his time, as if it was likely that he would be played at Italian or French courts in the years to come, in the sense in which Rameau certainly thought this, and that he was not in his own mind a pioneer and innovator, a lawgiver to others, as Rameau was; that he was only too pleased if works were played in his own city or at the courts of the German Princes; that his universe was, in other words, socially (not, of course, emotionally or artistically) bounded, in the way in which that of the Parisiens was not. This is a great irony of fate, since, as you rightly say, this towering genius, comparable to Shakespeare or Dante, did transcend his time, and is a major luminary of human civilisation in the way in which all these Frenchmen were not. In short, all I wished to say was that Bach, like other Germans of his time, was modest in his ambitions, and that this was an effect and a cause of the turning inwards which produced such immense spiritual results out of the very misery of German provincialism and lack of a sense of world importance in the eighteenth century.'

miserable human beings. What occurred was a kind of retreat in depth. It sometimes happens in human history – though parallels may be dangerous – that when the natural road towards human fulfilment is blocked, human beings retreat into themselves, become involved in themselves, and try to create inwardly that world which some evil fate has denied them externally. This is certainly what happened in Ancient Greece when Alexander the Great began to destroy the city-states, and the Stoics and the Epicureans began to preach a new morality of personal salvation, which took the form of saying that politics was unimportant, civil life was unimportant, all the great ideals held up by Pericles and by Demosthenes, by Plato and by Aristotle, were trivial and as nothing before the imperative need for personal individual salvation.

This was a very grand form of sour grapes. If you cannot obtain from the world that which you really desire, you must teach yourself not to want it. If you cannot get what you want, you must teach yourself to want what you *can* get. This is a very frequent form of spiritual retreat in depth, into a kind of inner citadel, in which you try to lock yourself up against all the fearful ills of the world. The king of my province – the prince – confiscates my land: I do not want to own land. The prince does not wish to give me rank: rank is trivial, unimportant. The king has robbed me of my possessions: possessions are nothing. My children have died of malnutrition and disease: earthly attachments, even love of children, are as nothing before love of God. And so forth. You gradually hedge yourself round with a kind of tight wall by which you seek to reduce your vulnerable surface – you want to be as little wounded as possible. Every kind of wound has been heaped upon you, and therefore you wish to contract yourself into the smallest possible area, so that as little of you as possible is exposed to further wounds.

This is the mood in which the German pietists operated. The result was an intense inner life, a great deal of very moving and very interesting but highly personal and violently emotional literature, hatred of the intellect, and above all, of course, violent hatred of France, of wigs, of silk stockings, of salons, of corruption, of generals, of emperors, of all the great and magnificent figures of this world, who are simply incarnations of wealth, wickedness and the devil. This is a natural reaction on the part of a pious and humiliated population, and has happened since their day in other places as well. It is a particular form of anti-culture, anti-intellectualism and xenophobia – to which the Germans were, at that particular moment, especially prone. This is the provincialism which some German thinkers cherished and adored in the eighteenth century, and against which Goethe and Schiller fought all their lives.

There is a typical quotation from Zinzendorf, the leader of the Herrnhuter, a sort of section of the Moravian Brotherhood, which was itself a large section of the pietist group. He said: 'Whoso wishes to grasp God with his intellect becomes an atheist.' This was simply an echo of Luther, who said that reason is a whore and must be avoided. Here a social fact about these Germans is not altogether irrelevant. If you ask who these Germans of the eighteenth century were, who were the thinkers who most influenced Germany and of whom we have heard, there is a rather peculiar sociological fact about them that supports the thesis which I wish to suggest, namely that the whole thing is a product of wounded national sensibility, of dreadful national humiliation, that this is the root of the romantic movement on the part of the Germans. If you ask who those thinkers were, you will find that, in contrast with the French, they came from an entirely different social milieu.

Lessing, Kant, Herder, Fichte were all very humbly born. Hegel, Schelling, Schiller, Hölderlin were lower middle-class. Goethe was a rich bourgeois but attained to a proper title only later. Only Kleist and Novalis were what would in those days be called country gentlemen. The only persons with any degree of aristocratic connection who could be said to take part in German literature, German life, German painting, any kind of German civilisation, as far as I could discover, were the two brothers the Counts Christian and Friedrich Leopold Stolberg, and the mystic Baron Carl von Eckertshausen – not exactly first-class figures, not exactly figures of the front rank.

If on the other hand you think about the French of this period, of all the radicals, the left wing, the most extreme opponents of orthodoxy, of the Church, of the monarchy, of the status quo, all these persons came from a very, very different world. Montesquieu was a baron, Condorcet was a marquis, Mably was an abbé, Condillac was an abbé, Buffon became a count, Volney was well-born. D'Alembert was the illegitimate son of a nobleman. Helvétius was not noble, but his father had been doctor to Madame and he was a millionaire, and a tax farmer, and moved in court circles. Baron Grimm and Baron d'Holbach were two Germans who came to live in Paris, one from near Bohemia, one from the Rhineland. There were a number of other abbés: the abbé Galiani was the Secretary at the Neapolitan Embassy; the abbé Morellet and the abbé Raynal were of good origin. Even Voltaire came from the minor gentry. Only Diderot and Rousseau were commoners, real commoners. Diderot really did come from the poor. Rousseau was a Swiss, and therefore does not count in this category. Consequently, these persons spoke with a different language. They were no doubt oppositional, but they were oppositional against persons who came from the same class as themselves. They went to salons, they glittered, they were persons of high polish, great education, splendid prose style and a generous and handsome outlook on life.

Their mere existence irritated, humiliated and infuriated the Germans. When Herder came to Paris in the early 1770s, he was unable to get into contact with any of these men. It appeared to him that they were all artificial, highly mannered, extremely self-conscious, dry, soulless little dancing-masters in salons who did not understand the inner life of man, who were debarred either by bad doctrine or by false origin from understanding the true purposes of men on earth and the true, rich, generous potentialities with which human beings had been endowed by God. This too helped to create a chasm between the Germans and the French – the mere thought of these *frondeurs*, the mere thought of this opposition, even on the part of those who themselves hated the Church of Rome, who themselves hated the King of France, filled them with nausea, disgust, humiliation and inferiority, and this dug an enormous ditch between the Germans and the French which not even all the cultural interchanges which can be traced by scholars were able to overcome. This is perhaps one of the roots of the German opposition to the French from which romanticism began.

There is one man who, in my view, struck the most violent blow against the Enlightenment and began the whole romantic process, the whole process of revolt against the outlook which I have tried to describe. He is an obscure figure, but obscure figures sometimes create great consequences. (Hitler too, after all, was an obscure man during a portion of his life.) Johann Georg Hamann was the son of very obscure parents. His father was a bath-keeper in the city of Königsberg, and he was brought up in East Prussia, in a pietist environment. He was a ne'er-do-well, he was not able to get a job, he wrote a little poetry, and a little criticism; he did it quite well, but not well enough to secure a living; he was supported by his neighbour and friend, Immanuel Kant, who lived in the same city, and with whom he quarrelled for the rest of his life; and then he was sent by some rich Baltic merchants to London, for the purpose of transacting a piece of business which he failed to complete, but instead drank, gambled and got into heavy debt.

As a result of these excesses he was near suicide, but then had a religious experience, read the Old Testament, which his pietist parents and grandparents had sworn by, and suddenly was spiritually transformed. He realised that the story of the Jews was the story of every man; that when he read the book of Ruth, or when he read the book of Job, or when he read about the tribulations of Abraham, God was speaking directly to his soul, and telling him that there were certain spiritual events which had an infinite significance far different from anything which might appear on the surface.

In this transformed religious condition he came back to Königsberg, and began to write. He wrote obscurely under many pseudonyms, and in a style which has proved from that day to this unreadable. At the same time he had a very powerful and marked influence upon a number of other writers, who in their turn had a considerable influence upon European life. He was admired by Herder, who certainly transformed the writing of history, and to some degree also initiated the whole attitude towards the arts which prevails today. He had an influence on Goethe, who wished to edit his works, and who regarded him as one of the most gifted and profound spirits of his time, and supported him against all possible rivals. He had an influence on Kierkegaard, who lived after Hamann died, and who said he was one of the profoundest writers he had ever read, even if he was not always intelligible, even to him. Nevertheless, although he wrote obscurely, it is possible by dint of extreme attention (which I do not really recommend) to collect certain grains of sense from the extraordinary contorted metaphors, euphuistic stylisms, allegories and other forms of dark poetical speech with which Hamann's fragmentary writings – he never finished anything – are written. The doctrine which he enunciated was approximately as follows.

He began with Hume, and said in effect that Hume was right; that if you ask yourself how it is that you know the universe, the answer is that you know it not by intellect, but by faith. If Hume said that he could not even eat an egg, he could not even drink a glass of water, without an act of faith which could not be bolstered up by logic, how much more was this true of almost every other experience we had. Hamann wished to say, of course, that his belief in God and in the Creation were bolstered by precisely the same argument as Hume's belief in his egg and his glass of water.

The French dealt in the general propositions of the sciences, but these general propositions never caught the actual living, palpitating reality of life. If you met a man and wished to know what he was like, to clap upon him various psychological and sociological generalisations gleaned from the works of Montesquieu or Condillac would teach you nothing. The only way to discover what human beings were like was by speaking to them, by communicating with them. Communication meant an actual meeting of two human beings, and by watching a man's face, and by watching the contortions of his body and his gestures, by hearing his words, and in many other ways which you could not afterwards analyse, you became convinced, a datum was presented to you, you knew to whom it was you were talking. Communication was established.

The attempt to analyse this communication into scientific, general propositions would of necessity fail. General propositions were baskets of an extremely crude kind. They were concepts and categories which differentiated that which was common to a great many things, common to many men of different sorts, common to many things of different sorts, common to various ages. What they left out, of necessity, because they were general, was that which was unique, that which was particular, that which was the specific property of this particular man, or this particular thing. And that alone was of interest, according to Hamann. If you wished to read a book, you were not interested in what this book had in common with many other books. If you looked at a picture, you did not wish to know what principles had gone into the making of this picture, principles which had also gone into the making of a thousand other pictures in a thousand other ages by a thousand different painters. You wished to react directly, to the specific message, to the specific reality, which looking at this picture, reading this book, speaking to this man, praying to this god would convey to you.

From this he drew a kind of Bergsonian conclusion, namely that there was a flow of life, and that the attempt to cut this flow into segments killed it. The sciences were very well for their own purposes. If you wished to discover about how to grow plants (and even then not always correctly); if you wished to know about some kind of general principles, about the general properties of bodies in general, whether physical or chemical; if you wished to know what climates would assist what kind of growth to develop in them, and so forth; then, no doubt, the sciences were very well. But this is not what men ultimately sought. If you asked yourself what were men after, what did men really want, you would see that what they wanted was not at all what Voltaire supposed they wanted. Voltaire thought that they wanted happiness, contentment, peace, but this was not true. What men wanted was for all their faculties to play in the richest and most violent possible fashion. What men wanted was to create, what men wanted was to make, and if this making led to clashes, if it led to wars, if it led to struggles, then this was part of the human lot. A man who had been put in a Voltairean garden, pared and pruned, who had been brought up by some wise *philosophe* in knowledge of physics and chemistry and mathematics, and in knowledge of all the sciences which the Encyclopaedists had recommended – such a man would be a form of death in life.

The sciences, if they were applied to human society, would lead to a kind of fearful bureaucratisation, he thought. He was against scientists, bureaucrats, persons who made things tidy, smooth Lutheran clergymen, deists, everybody who wanted to put things in boxes, everybody who wished to assimilate one thing to another, who wished to prove, for example, that creation was really the same as the obtaining of certain data which nature provides and their rearrangement in certain pleasing patterns – whereas for Hamann, of course, creation was a most ineffable, indescribable, unanalysable personal act, by which a human being laid his stamp on nature, allowed his will to soar, spoke his word, uttered that which was within him and which would not brook any kind of obstacle. Therefore the whole of the Enlightenment doctrine appeared to him to kill that which was living in human beings, appeared to offer a pale substitute for the creative energies of man, and for the whole rich world of the senses, without which it is impossible for human beings to live, to eat, to drink, to be merry, to meet other people, to indulge in a thousand and one acts without which people wither and die. It seemed to him that the Enlightenment laid no stress on that, that the human being as painted by Enlightenment thinkers was, if not 'economic man', at any rate some kind of artificial toy, some kind of lifeless model, which had no relation to the kind of human beings whom Hamann met and wished to associate with every day of his life.

Goethe says much the same thing about Moses Mendelssohn. He says Mendelssohn treats beauty as entomologists treat butterflies. He catches the poor animal, he pins it down, and as its exquisite colours drop off, there it lies, a lifeless corpse under the pin. This is aesthetics! This is a very typical reaction on the part of the youthful, romantic Goethe of the 1770s, under the influence of Hamann, against the tendency on the part of the French to generalise, to classify, to pin down, to arrange in albums, to try to produce some kind of rational ordering of human experience, leaving out the *élan vital*, the flow, the individuality, the desire to create, the desire, even, to struggle, that element in human beings which produced a creative clash of opinion between people of different views, instead of that dead harmony and peace which, according to Hamann and his followers, the French were after.

That is how Hamann began. Let me quote some typical passages to illustrate his approach. The bliss of the human soul, says Hamann, is not at all what Voltaire seems to think, namely happiness. The bliss of the human soul is rooted in the untrammelled realisation of its powers. As man is made in God's image, so is the body a picture of the soul. This is quite an interesting view. The body is a picture of the soul, because when you meet a human being, and you say 'What is he like?', you judge by his face. You judge by his body, and the idea that there are a soul and a body which can be dissected, that there are spirit and flesh which are different, that the body is one thing, but there is something inside the man, a kind of ghost palpitating inside this machine, which is quite different from what the man is in his totality, in his unity, is a typical dissecting French view. 'What is this highly praised *reason*, with its universality, infallibility, overweeningness, certainty, self-evidence? It is a stuffed dummy which the *howling* superstition of unreason has endowed with *divine attributes*.' The abbé Dubos at the beginning of the eighteenth century said: 'What one has felt and thought in one language one can express with equal elegance in any other.' This to Hamann was absolute madness. Language is that with which we express ourselves. There is no such thing as thought on the one hand, and language on the other. Language is not a glove which we put on our thought. When we think, we think in symbols, we think in words, and therefore all translation is in principle impossible. Those who think, think in particular symbols, and these symbols are the ones which strike upon the senses and the imagination of the people to whom we speak. Approximations may be made in other languages, but if you really wish to enter into contact with human beings, if you really wish to understand what they think, what they feel and what they are, then you must understand every gesture, every nuance, you must watch their eyes, you must observe the movement of their lips, you must hear their words, you must understand their handwriting, and then you come to direct acquaintance with the actual sources of life. Anything less than that, the attempt to translate a man's language into another language, to classify all his various movements by some anatomical or physiognomical means, to try to put him into a box with a lot of other people and produce a learned volume which will simply classify him as one of a species, one of a type, that is the way to miss all knowledge, that is the way to kill, that is the way to apply concepts and categories, hollow baskets, to the palpitating, unique, asymmetrical, unclassifiable flesh of living human experience.

This, roughly speaking, is the doctrine of Hamann; and it is the doctrine which he bequeathed to his followers. To abolish caprice and fancy in the arts, he said, is to be like an assassin, plotting against the arts, life and honour. Passion – that is what art possesses; passion, which cannot be described and cannot be classified. That, he says, is what Moses Mendelssohn, that aesthetic Moses – Moses the aesthetic lawgiver – wants to circumcise with all these aesthetic commandments: thou shalt not assail this, thou shalt not taste that. In a free State, he says, where the leaves from the divine book of the divine Shakespeare blow about in all the tempests of time, how dare a man do this?

Goethe said about Hamann: 'In order to achieve the impossible he stretches his hand to all the elements.' And he summarised Hamann's outlook in this way: 'All that a man undertakes . . . must spring from his united powers, all separation is to be rejected.'

3

THE TRUE FATHERS OF ROMANTICISM

MY REASON for having introduced the obscure figure of Johann
Georg Hamann is that I believe him to have been the first person
to declare war upon the Enlightenment in the most open, violent
and complete fashion. Nevertheless, he was not entirely alone in
this, even in his own lifetime. Let me explain why I say this.

The eighteenth century, as everybody knows – this is a platitude
– was the age of the great triumph of science. The great victories of
science are the most phenomenal event of that period; and the most
profound revolution in human sentiment which occurred in that
age was the result of the destruction of older forms – the result of
the attack both upon the established religion on the part of
organised natural science, and upon the old medieval hierarchy by
the new secular State.

At the same time, without doubt, the rationalism went so far
that, as always happens in such cases, the human sentiment which
is blocked by rationalism of this type sought for some kind of
egress in other directions. When the Olympian gods become too
tame, too rational and too normal, people naturally enough begin
to incline towards darker, more chthonian deities. This is what
happened in the third century BC in Greece, and what began
happening in the eighteenth century.

There is no doubt that organised religion was on the retreat.
Consider for example the kind of rational religion which was
preached by the disciples of Leibniz in Germany, where the great
philosopher Wolff, who dominated German universities, tried to
reconcile religion with reason. Anything which could not be
reconciled with reason became unfashionable, so that it was
necessary to save religion by proving its harmony with reason.

Wolff tried to do this by saying that miracles could be reconciled with a rational interpretation of the universe, by supposing, for example, that when Joshua stopped the sun at Jericho he was simply an astrophysicist with more profound knowledge than most other astrophysicists of his time, and that this degree, this depth of penetration, of astrophysical knowledge on his part was certainly miraculous. Similarly, when Christ turned water into wine he simply understood chemistry in a more profound manner than that in which any human being not assisted by divine inspiration could have understood it.

Given that this is the depth to which rationalism had fallen, and that religion had to make this kind of compromise in order to have any opportunity of being accepted at all, it is perhaps not very surprising that people should have turned elsewhere for moral and spiritual satisfaction. There is no doubt that, while perhaps happiness and order might be provided by the new scientific philosophy, the irrational desires of men, the whole realm of those unconscious drives of which the twentieth century has made us so very acutely aware, began to breed some kind of satisfactions of their own. So, perhaps somewhat to the surprise of people who believe the eighteenth century to have been a harmonious, symmetrical, infinitely rational, elegant, glassy sort of century, a kind of peaceful mirror of human reason and human beauty not disturbed by anything deeper or darker, we find that never in the history of Europe had so many irrational persons wandered over its surface claiming adherence. It is in the eighteenth century that the Masonic and the Rosicrucian sects thrive. It is then that all kinds of charlatans and wanderers begin to have an appeal – particularly in the second half of the century. It is then that Cagliostro appears in Paris and gets involved in the highest circles. It is then that Mesmer begins talking about animal spirits. This is the favoured age of all kinds of necromancers and chiromancers and hydromancers, whose various nostrums engage the attention and indeed capture the faith of a great many otherwise apparently sane and rational persons. Certainly the experiments in the occult of the Kings of Sweden and of Denmark, of the Duchess of Devonshire and of the Cardinal de Rohan, would have been surprising in the seventeenth century, and unknown in the nineteenth. It is the eighteenth century in which these things begin to spread.

There were of course more respectable and interesting manifestations of the same anti-rationalism. For example Lavater in Zurich, a kind of Jung of his day, invented the science of what he called 'Physiognomik'. He attempted to measure people's faces for the purpose of obtaining some kind of insight into their psychological character, because of a belief in the unity and indissolubility of the spiritual and the physical aspects of men. At the same time, he did not discourage all those much more dubious phrenologists and spiritualists of one kind or another, all those strange Messiahs who wandered about, occasionally committing crimes, at other times merely causing stupefaction, some of whom were arrested for their crimes, while others were allowed to roam about at large in, for example, the wilder and more old-fashioned portions of the German empire.

At any rate, this is the atmosphere in which we move, so that under the surface of this apparently coherent, apparently elegant century there are all kinds of dark forces moving. Hamann is merely the most poetical, theologically the most profound, and the most interesting representative of this violent revolt of, as we might put it, quality against quantity, of all the anti-scientific yearnings and desires of men. Hamann's fundamental doctrine, which I have already tried to summarise, was that God was not a geometer, not a mathematician, but a poet; that there was something blasphemous in attempting to foist upon God our own puny, human, logical schemes. When his friend Kant said to him that the science of astronomy had finally come to an end, that astronomers knew all they could know and it was a satisfactory thing that this particular science could now be locked up as having been completed, Hamann felt like destroying it. As if there would be no more miracles in the universe! As if any human endeavour could be regarded as over and done with, finished! The very notion that human beings were finite, that there were certain subjects about which everything could be known, that there was some portion of nature which could be fully investigated, and some questions which could be ultimately answered, all this appeared to Hamann to be shocking, unreal and plainly stupid.

This is the heart of Hamann's doctrine. It is a kind of mystical vitalism which perceives in nature and in history the voice of God. That the voice of God speaks to us through nature was an old mystical belief. Hamann added to this the further doctrine that history too speaks to us, that all the various historical events which are simply taken to be ordinary empirical events by unenlightened historians are really methods whereby the Divine speaks to us. Each of these events possesses an occult or mystical significance which those with eyes to see can perceive. He was among the earliest – later than Vico, but Vico was not read – of those who said that myths were not simply false statements about the world, neither the wicked inventions of unscrupulous persons, seeking to throw dust in people's eyes, nor pretty embellishments invented by poets for the purpose of decorating their wares. Myths were ways in which human beings expressed their sense of the ineffable, inexpressible mysteries of nature, and there was no other way in which it could be expressed. If words were used, they did not do their job properly. Words cut things to pieces too much. Words classified, words were too rational. The attempt to tie things up into neat parcels and arrange them in some beautifully analytic fashion destroyed the unity, the continuity and the vitality of the subject-matter – that is to say life and the world – which you were contemplating. Myths conveyed this mystery in artistic images and artistic symbols, which, without words, managed to connect man with the mysteries of nature. This, roughly speaking, was the doctrine.

The whole thing was of course an immense protest against the French. It spread beyond Germany. Phenomena of this kind are noticeable in England also, where the most eloquent exponent of this point of view, somewhat later than Hamann, is the mystical poet William Blake. Blake's enemies, the persons whom he regards as the villains of the whole modern period, are Locke and Newton. Them he regards as those devils who killed the spirit by cutting reality into some kind of mathematically symmetrical pieces, whereas reality is a living whole which can be appreciated only in some non-mathematical fashion. He was a typical Swedenborgian, and Swedenborg's disciples were very typical of the kind of occult subterranean movements in the eighteenth century which I have referred to.

What Blake, like all mystics of his type, desired was some kind of recovery of control over the spiritual element, which had become petrified as a result of human degeneration and the wicked work of unimaginative killers of the human spirit such as mathematicians and scientists. There are a number of quotations which convey this. Blake says that laws are needed to fence men off:

> And their children wept, & built
> Tombs in the desolate places,
> And form'd laws of prudence, and call'd them
> The eternal laws of God.

This is directed against the rationalists of the eighteenth century and the whole notion of symmetrically arranged order founded upon non-mystical empirical or logical reasoning. When he writes in those famous lines which everyone knows:

> A Robin Red breast in a Cage
> Puts all Heaven in a Rage,

the cage of which he speaks is the Enlightenment, and that is the cage in which he and persons like him appeared to suffocate all their lives in the second half of the eighteenth century.

> Children of the future Age,
> Reading this indignant page;
> Know that in a former time,
> Love! sweet Love! was thought a crime.

Love to him was identical with art. Jesus he calls an artist; his disciples he also calls artists. 'Art is the Tree of Life ... Science is the Tree of Death.' Liberate the spark – that is the great cry of all persons who feel strangled and suffocated by the new tidy scientific order which does not respond to the deeper problems that agitate the human soul.

The Germans tended to suppose that in France nobody was aware, nobody began to be aware, of what these deeper problems were; that the French were all desiccated monkeys, with no conception of what it was that moved human beings, at any rate human beings as possessors of souls, as possessors of some kind of spiritual needs. This was not entirely true. If, for example, you read even such a representative thinker of the Enlightenment as Diderot, upon whom the Germans in question looked as one of the most noxious representatives of the new materialism, the new science, the new destruction of all that was spiritual and religious in life, you will find something that is not all that unlike even the attitude among the Germans which I have described. Diderot is perfectly aware that there is such a thing as the irrational element in man, that there are unconscious depths in which all kinds of dark forces move, and he is aware that human genius feeds upon these, and that the forces of light are not by themselves enough to create those divine works of art which he himself admires. He speaks of art, very often, in tones of great passion, and says that there is about the great genius, the great artist, something, a *je ne sais quoi* (a seventeenth-century expression), which enables the artist to create these works of art in his imagination with a degree of sweep, with a magnificent depth of insight, and with a degree of intellectual courage – the taking of huge intellectual risks – which makes men of genius and artists of this type akin to great criminals. There is a passage in Diderot where he speculates upon the nearness to criminals of artists, because they both defy rules, they are both persons who are in love with power, magnificence and splendour, and kick over the traces of normal life, and the whole tame existence of over-civilised man.

Diderot is among the first to preach that there are two men. There is the artificial man, who belongs in society and conforms to the practices of society and seeks to please; he is the normal sort of artificial, mincing little figure of the caricaturists of the eighteenth century. Within this man, however, there is imprisoned the violent, bold, dark, criminal instinct of a man who wishes to break out. This is the man who, if properly controlled, is responsible for magnificent works of genius. Genius of this type cannot be tamed, genius of this type has nothing to do with those rules which the abbé Batteux or the abbé Dubos laid down as being the rational conventions, the rational rules, in accordance with which alone good works of art can be produced. In a typical passage in the *Salon* of 1765, one of the early works of art criticism for which he is justly famous, Diderot writes:

> Beware of those whose pockets are full of *esprit* – of wit – and who scatter this wit at every opportunity, everywhere. They have no demon within them, they are not gloomy, or sombre, or melancholy, or silent. They are never either awkward or foolish. The lark, the chaffinch, the linnet, the canary, they chirp and twitter all the livelong day, at sunset they fold their head under their wing, and lo! they are asleep. It is then that genius takes his lamp and lights it. And this dark, solitary, savage bird, this untamable creature, with its gloomy melancholy plumage, opens its throat and begins its song, makes the groves resound and breaks the silence and the darkness of the night.

This is a paean to genius, in contrast with talent, in contrast with rules, in contrast with the vaunted so-called virtues of the eighteenth century – sanity, rationality, measure, proportion and all the rest of it. It shows that even in this terrible desiccated city of Paris, where according to the Germans nobody has ever lived, nobody has ever seen a colour, nobody has ever known what a stirring of the human soul is, nobody has any notion of what the agonies of the spirit are, what God is, or what the transfiguration of man may be – in this very city there were persons who were aware of self-transcendence, of irrational forces, of something undoubtedly of the same type as that which Hamann sang forth.

Here it will again be asked: What about Rousseau? The point is well taken. It would be foolish to deny that Rousseau's doctrine, Rousseau's words, were among the factors which influenced the romantic movement. Nevertheless, again I have to repeat: His role has been exaggerated. If we consider what it is that Rousseau actually said, as opposed to the manner in which he said it – and the manner and the life are what are important – we find that it is the purest milk of the rationalist word. All that Rousseau said is this: We live in a corrupt society; we live in a bad, hypocritical society, where men lie to each other and murder each other and are false to each other. It is possible to discover the truth. This truth is to be discovered not by means of sophistication or Cartesian logic but by looking within the heart of the simple uncorrupt human being, the noble savage, or the child, or whoever it may be. Once this truth is discovered, it is an eternal truth, true for all men, everywhere, in all climes and seasons, and when we have discovered this truth, then it is important that we should live in accordance with it. This is not different from what the Hebrew prophets have said, or from what has been said by every Christian preacher who has ever preached against the corrupt sophistication of the big cities, and the falling away from God which occurs in such places.

Rousseau's actual doctrine is not very different from that of the Encyclopaedists. He disliked them personally, because temperamentally he was a kind of dervish from the desert. He was paranoiac, savage and gloomy in some respects, and highly neurotic, as we should say today; therefore he did not have much in common with the people at Holbach's rather irreverent table or at the elegant receptions which Voltaire held at Ferney. But this was to a certain degree a personal or emotional matter. The actual substance of what Rousseau said was not so very different from the official enlightened doctrine of the eighteenth century. What was different was the manner; what was different was the temperament. When Rousseau begins describing his own particular states of mind and states of soul, when he begins describing the emotions which tear him apart, the violent paroxysms of rage or joy through which he goes, then he does use a tone which is very different from that of the eighteenth century. But this is not the doctrine of Rousseau which was inherited by the Jacobins, or which in various forms entered into the doctrines of the nineteenth century.

There are passages which do entitle him to be regarded as one of the fathers of romanticism. For example: 'I did not reason, I did not philosophise ... ravished I surrendered to the confusion of these great ideas ... I suffocated in the universe, I wanted to leap into the infinite ... my spirit gave itself to swelling ecstasy.' That kind of passage is not very similar to the more sober or saner passages of the Encyclopaedists; it would not have been cared for by Helvétius or by Holbach or by Voltaire, or even by Diderot. Rousseau's point was that nobody could love as Rousseau loved, nobody could hate as Rousseau hated, nobody could suffer as Rousseau suffered, and only Rousseau could understand Rousseau.

He was unique. Nobody else could understand him, and only a genius could understand another genius. This was a doctrine opposed to the view that the truth was equally open to all reasonable men who did not becloud their understandings with unnecessary emotions and unnecessary ignorance. What Rousseau does is to contrast with the so-called cold logic which he constantly complains about, with cold reason, the hot tears of shame, of joy or misery, or love, or despair, or mortification, or spiritual agony, or ecstatic vision, and that is why Hamann called him the best of the sophists – but still a sophist. Hamann was Socrates and Rousseau was a sophist; he was the best because he gave signs of understanding that all was not quite right with this elegant, rational, sane Paris.

Rousseau was still a sophist because his doctrines still appealed to reason; they still appealed to the fact that there was some kind of establishment, some kind of good human life, good men. If only they would scrape off all the falsehood which had managed to accumulate upon them through the centuries, if only they could remove the bad society which had corrupted them, then they could live well for ever, in accordance with timeless precepts. That is precisely what the Germans disbelieved, precisely what they rightly accused Rousseau of believing. The only difference was that the other Encyclopaedists in Paris believed this could be achieved by reform, gradually, by somehow converting the rulers to their point of view, by getting hold of an enlightened despot so that, if he was enlightened enough, he could establish some kind of better life on earth. Rousseau believed that the whole cursed superstructure must be razed to the ground, that the entire wicked human society must be burnt to ashes; then a new phoenix would arise, constructed by himself and by his disciples. But in principle what Rousseau and the other Encyclopaedists wished to do was the same, although perhaps their view of the appropriate methods may have differed.

If we compare this kind of talk with what the Germans were saying at the same time, we will see that the German attitude towards all this is far more violent. There is a typical passage in the poet Lenz, who committed suicide. He was an approximate contemporary of Rousseau. He said:

Action, action is the soul of the world, not pleasure, not abandonment to feeling, not abandonment to reasoning, only action; only by action does one become the image of God, the God who creates ceaselessly and ceaselessly rejoices in his works. Without action, all pleasure, all feeling, all knowledge is nothing but a postponed death. We must not cease from toil until we have created free space, even if this space is a fearful waste and a fearful void, and then we shall brood over it, as God brooded over the waste and the void before the world was created, and then something will arise. O bliss, O godlike feeling!

This is something of a very different order from even the most violent lucubrations, the most ecstatic exclamations of Rousseau, and indicates a very different attitude. This sudden passion for action as such, this hatred of any established order, hatred of any kind of view of the universe as having a structure which calm (or even uncalm) perception is able to understand, contemplate, classify, describe and finally use – this is unique to the Germans.

As for its causes, I can only repeat my previous suggestion, namely that it was largely due both to the intense spirituality of the pietism from which these people spring, and to the ravages of science, which undermined their pietistic faith and, while leaving them with the temperament of pietists, had removed the religious certainties of that movement.

If you look at the plays, the fourth- and fifth- and sixth-rate plays, which the so-called Storm and Stress movement in Germany produced in the 1760s and 1770s, you will there find a very different tone from that prevailing anywhere else in European literature. Take Klinger, a German playwright who wrote a play called *Sturm und Drang* ('Storm and Stress'), after which the movement is called. There is a play by Klinger called *The Twins* in which one of the twins, a more powerful, imaginative and fiery romantic, kills his weak, priggish and disagreeable brother, because, he says, his brother will not let him develop his nature in accordance with his demonic or titanic demands. In all previous tragedies the assumption was that in some other society there would be no need for these dreadful things to occur. Society is bad, therefore it must be improved. Men are done down by society; well then, one must be able to imagine a better society, as Rousseau was able to imagine it, in which people do not suffocate, in which people do not fight, in which the bad are not at the top and the good at the bottom, in which parents do not torture their children, in which women are not married off to men they do not love. It must be possible to construct a better world. Not so in Klinger's tragedy, not so in *Julius von Tarent*, a tragedy by Leisewitz.

I do not wish to recite any more of these justly forgotten names, but broadly speaking the substance of all these plays is that there is some kind of insoluble conflict in the world, in nature itself, as a result of which the strong cannot live with the weak, the lions cannot live with the lambs. The strong must have room in which to breathe, and the weak go to the wall; if the weak suffer, they will naturally resist, and it is right that they should resist, and it is right that the strong should suppress them. Therefore conflict, collision, tragedy, death – all kinds of horrors – are inevitably involved in the nature of the universe. The view is therefore fatalistic and pessimistic, not scientific and optimistic, not even spiritual and optimistic, in any sense of the word.

This attitude has a kind of natural affinity to Hamann's view that God is closer to the abnormal than he is to the normal, which he openly says: the normal do not really understand what goes on. This is an original moment at which the whole Dostoevsky complex comes into existence. In a certain sense, of course, it is an application of Christianity, but a rather new one, because so sincere and so deeply intended. On this view God is closer to the thieves and the prostitutes, the sinners and the publicans, than he is (Hamann says) to the smooth philosophers of Paris, or the smooth clergymen in Berlin who are trying to reconcile religion with reason, which is degradation and humiliation of everything that man cares for. All the great masters who excel in human endeavour, says Hamann, were sick men in one way or another, had wounds – Hercules, Ajax, Socrates, St Paul, Solon, the Hebrew prophets, Bacchantes, demonic figures – none of these were men of good sense. That, I think, lies at the heart of the whole violent doctrine of personal self-assertion which is the core of the German 'Storm and Stress'.

However, all these dramatists are comparatively minor figures. I bring them in merely in order to show that Hamann, who I think does justly deserve to be rescued from the darkness of oblivion, was not entirely alone. The only worthwhile, valuable work which the *Sturm und Drang* produced was *Werther* by Goethe, a typical expression of its author. There, too, there is no cure. There is no way in which Werther can avoid suicide, there is no situation in which Werther, being in love with a married lady, and the marriage vow being what it is, and believed by Werther and by the lady herself to be what it is – there is no way in which this problem can be solved. If one man's love and another man's love come into collision, it is a hopeless and helpless business, and must end badly. That is the moral of *Werther*, and that is why young men up and down Germany were said to have committed suicide in its name – not because in the eighteenth century or in their particular society there was no adequate solution, but because they despaired of the world and thought it an irrational place, in which a solution was in principle undiscoverable.

This, then, is the atmosphere which developed in Germany in the 1760s and 1770s. But there were two men who were in my view the true fathers of romanticism. They were certainly of vaster size than any of the people I have mentioned hitherto as being responsible for it, and to them I must now turn. They both emerged from this movement, one sympathetic to it, the other acutely hostile to it but by his work a greater advancer of its ideals, as sometimes ironically happens. The first is Herder, the second is Kant, and on them I must dwell a little.

I do not wish to expound the general ideas and the new notions for which Herder is responsible, and by which he transformed, for example, our notions of history, our notions of society, so vast was the influence which this extraordinary thinker had. He too was a pietist and a Prussian, and like the others revolted against the spick and span empire of Frederick the Great. It was this tidy, enlightened despotism – and it was enlightened – managed by French intellectuals and French officials under the leadership of this extremely clear-headed, energetic, powerful despot, that caused these good men to suffocate – even Kant, let alone Herder, who was by nature of a somewhat irascible and unbalanced temperament. The doctrines of Herder on which I wish to focus are three. They are doctrines which contributed very powerfully to the romantic movement and which arose quite naturally out of the milieu which I have described. One is the notion of what I shall call expressionism; the second is the notion of belonging, what it means to belong to a group; and the third is the notion that ideals – true ideals – are often incompatible with one another and cannot be reconciled. These three ideas each had a revolutionary significance in their day, and are worth lingering over a little because they are commonly not done justice to, even in primers of the history of thought.

The first notion, of expressionism, is this. Herder believed that one of the fundamental functions of human beings was to express, to speak, and therefore that whatever a man did expressed his full nature; and if it did not express his full nature, it was because he maimed himself, or restrained himself, or laid some kind of leash upon his energies. This he learned from his master Hamann. Herder really was a direct and faithful disciple of this strange figure, who was called 'der Magus in Norden', the Magus in the North – 'Magus' in the same sense as in 'the three Magi'.

In the aesthetics of the eighteenth century – even the much more passionate aesthetics of someone like Diderot as compared with the dry and conventional aesthetics of the abbé Batteux – broadly speaking, the value of a work of art would be said to consist in its being what it was. So the value of a picture was that it was beautiful. What made it beautiful one could argue about; whether it was because it gave pleasure, whether it was because it satisfied the intellect, whether it was because it had some peculiar relation to the harmonies of the spheres or of the universe, and was a copy of some great Platonic original, to which the artist in a moment of inspiration had access – about that you might disagree. What everyone agreed about was that the value of a work of art consisted in the properties which it had, its being what it was – beautiful, symmetrical, shapely, whatever it might be. A silver bowl was beautiful because it was a beautiful bowl, because it had the properties of being beautiful, however that is defined. This had nothing to do with who made it, and it had nothing to do with why it was made. The artist took very much the position of a purveyor who said: My private life is no business of the man who buys the work of art; you have asked for a silver bowl, here it is, I provide it. It is no business of yours whether I am a good husband or a good voter, or a nice man, or believe in God. You have asked for a table, here is a table; if it is a solid, sound table, such as you need, what complaints can you have? You have asked for a painting, you have asked for a portrait; if it is a good portrait, take it. I am Mozart, I am Haydn, I hope to produce a beautiful musical composition, by which I mean one which will be recognised as beautiful by others, and for which I shall be paid an adequate commission, and which will perhaps make my name as an immortal artist. That is the normal eighteenth-century view, and it is the view of a great many people, indeed probably the majority, since.

This was not the view which the Germans with whom we are concerned took, particularly not Hamann's view, and certainly not Herder's. For them a work of art is the expression of somebody, it is always a voice speaking. A work of art is the voice of one man addressing himself to other men. Whether it be a silver bowl or a musical composition, or a poem, or even a code of laws – whatever it might be, any artefact of human hands is in some way the expression of the attitude to life, conscious or unconscious, of its maker. When we appreciate a work of art, we are put in some kind of contact with the man who made it, and it speaks to us; that is the doctrine. Therefore the idea that an artist should say, 'As an artist I do this, and as a voter or husband I do that', the very notion that I can chop myself up into compartments and say that with one hand I do one thing, and this has nothing to do with what my other hand is doing, that my private convictions have nothing to do with the speeches which I put into the mouths of the characters in my tragedy, that I am simply a purveyor, that what must be judged is the work of art and not the maker, that the biography, the psychology, the purposes, the whole substance of the artist is irrelevant to the work of art – that doctrine was rejected with violence by Herder and by those who followed him. Take, for example, folk song. If a folk song speaks to you, they said, it is because the people who made it were Germans like yourself, and they spoke to you, who belong with them in the same society; and because they were Germans they used particular nuances, they used particular successions of sounds, they used particular words which, being in some way connected, and swimming on the great tide of words and symbols and experience upon which all Germans swim, have something peculiar to say to certain persons which they cannot say to certain other persons. The Portuguese cannot understand the inwardness of a German song as a German can, and a German cannot understand the inwardness of a Portuguese song, and the very fact that there is such a thing as inwardness at all in these songs is an argument for supposing that these are not simply objects like objects in nature, which do not speak; they are artefacts, that is to say, something which a man has made for the purpose of communicating with another man.

This is the doctrine of art as expression, the doctrine of art as communication. Herder goes on from this to develop the thesis in the most poetical and imaginative manner. He says that some things are made by individuals, and other things are made by groups. Some things are made consciously, and other things are made unconsciously. If you ask who has made folk song, who has made folk dancing, who has made the German laws, who has made German morals, who has made the institutions under which we live, you cannot give the answer; this lies shrouded in the mists of impersonal antiquity; nevertheless, men have made these things. The world is what men have made of it; our world, our German world, is constructed by other Germans, and that is why it smells and feels and looks and sounds to us as it does. From this he developed the notion that every man seeks to belong to some kind of group, or in fact does belong to it, and if taken out of it will feel alien and not at home. The whole notion of being at home, or being cut off from one's natural roots, the whole idea of roots, the whole idea of belonging to a group, a sect, a movement, was invented largely by Herder. There are anticipations of this in Vico's marvellous work, the *New Science*, but (I repeat) this had been forgotten, and although Herder might have seen it in the late 1770s, he appears to have developed most of his ideas before any date at which he is likely to have seen this work by his great Italian predecessor.

Herder's fundamental conviction was something of this order. Every man who wishes to express himself uses words. Words are not his invention, they are already passed on to him in some kind of inherited stream of traditional images. This stream has itself been fed by other men expressing themselves. A man has more in common, of an impalpable kind, with other men with whom nature has placed him in some proximity than he has with men remote from him. Herder does not use the criterion of blood, and he does not use the criterion of race. He talks about the nation, but the German word *Nation* in the eighteenth century did not have the connotation of 'nation' in the nineteenth. He speaks of language as a bond, and he speaks of soil as a bond, and the thesis, roughly speaking, is this: That which people who belong to the same group have in common is more directly responsible for their being as they are than that which they have in common with others in other places. To wit, the way in which, let us say, a German rises and sits down, the way in which he dances, the way in which he legislates, his handwriting and his poetry and his music, the way in which he combs his hair and the way in which he philosophises all have some impalpable common gestalt. All have some pattern quality in virtue of which they are recognisable as German, both by him and by others, wherein they differ from similar acts on the part of the Chinese. The Chinese also comb their hair, they also write poetry, they also have laws, they also hunt and obtain their food in various ways and make their clothing. There is also something common, of course, to the ways in which all men react to similar natural stimuli. Nevertheless there is a peculiar gestalt quality which qualifies certain human groups – not nationalities, perhaps; perhaps these groups are smaller. Herder was certainly not a nationalist in the sense of believing that there was some kind of deep impalpable essence to do with blood or race – all he believed was that human groups grew in some plant-like or some animal-like fashion, and that organic, botanical and other biological metaphors were more suitable for describing such growth than were the chemical and mathematical metaphors of the French eighteenth-century popularisers of science.

From this certain romantic conclusions do follow; that is to say, conclusions which affected anti-rationalism at least as it was understood in the eighteenth century. The principal one for our present purposes is this: that if indeed this is so then it clearly follows that objects cannot be described without reference to the purposes of their makers. The value of a work of art has to be analysed in terms of the particular group of persons to whom it is addressed, the motive of him who speaks, the effect upon those who are spoken to, and the bond which it automatically creates between the speaker and the spoken to. It is a form of communication, and if it is a form of communication then it has not got an impersonal or eternal value. If you wish to understand a work of art made by some ancient Greek, it is no use laying down timeless criteria in terms of which all works of art must be beautiful and then considering whether the Greek work of art is beautiful or not in terms of these criteria. Unless you understand what the Greeks were, what they wanted, how they lived, unless (as Herder says, echoing Vico in the most uncanny way) by an act of the most enormous difficulty, with the greatest possible effort of the imagination, you enter into the feelings of these exceedingly strange peoples, remote from you in time and place, unless you try by some act of imagination to reconstruct within yourself the form of life which these people led, what their laws were, what their ethical principles were, what their streets looked like, what their various values were, unless you try in other words to live yourself into their form of life – all this is commonplace now, but was not commonplace in the 1760s and 1770s when it was first spoken – unless you try to do that, your chances of truly understanding their art and truly understanding their writings and really knowing what Plato meant and really knowing who Socrates was are small. Socrates for Herder is not the timeless sage of the French Enlightenment, the timeless rationalist sage, nor is he simply the ironical deflator of pompous know-alls, which is what Hamann conceived him to be. Socrates is a fifth-century Athenian who lived in fifth-century Athens – not in the fourth century, not in the second, not in Germany, not in France, but in Greece, then and only then. In order to understand Greek philosophy, you must understand Greek art; in order to understand Greek art you must understand Greek history; in order to understand Greek history, you must understand Greek geography, you must see the plants which the Greeks saw, you must understand the soil on which they lived, and so on and so on.

This therefore becomes the beginning of the whole notion of historicism, evolutionism, the very notion that you can understand other human beings only in terms of an environment very dissimilar to your own. This is also the root of the notion of belonging. This notion is really elucidated for the first time by Herder, and that is why the whole idea of cosmopolitan man, a man who is equally at home in Paris, or Copenhagen, or Iceland, or India, is, to him, repellent. A man belongs to where he is, people have roots, they can create only in terms of those symbols in which they were brought up, and they were brought up in terms of some kind of closed society which spoke to them in a uniquely intelligible fashion. Any man who has not had the good fortune to suffer this, any man who was brought up without roots, on a desert island, by himself, in exile, an *émigré*, is to that extent weakened, and his creative powers are automatically made the smaller. This was not a doctrine which could have been understood, and certainly not one which could have been approved of, by the rationalist, universalist, objectivist cosmopolitan thinkers of the French eighteenth century.

But a far more startling conclusion follows from this, which Herder did not perhaps himself altogether stress, and that is this. If the value of every culture resides in what that particular culture seeks after – as he says, every culture has its own centre of gravity – you must determine what this centre of gravity, the *Schwerpunkt* as he calls it, is before you can even understand what these men were about; it is no use judging these things from the point of view of some other century or some other culture. If you have to do that then you will grasp the fact that different ages had different ideals, and these ideals were each in its way valid for its time and its place, and can be admired and appreciated by us now.

But now consider: at the outset I tried to establish that one of the great axioms of the eighteenth-century Enlightenment, which is what romanticism came to destroy, was that valid, objective answers could be discovered to all the great questions which agitate mankind – how to live, what to be, what is good, what is bad, what is right, what is wrong, what is beautiful, what is ugly, why act thus rather than thus – and that these answers can be obtained by some special method recommended by the particular thinker in question, and that all these answers can be stated in the form of propositions, and all these propositions, if they are true, will be compatible with one another – perhaps even more than compatible, perhaps they will even entail one another – and taken together these propositions will constitute that ideal, perfect state of affairs which for one reason or another we should all like to see happen, whether or not it is actually practicable or feasible.

But now suppose that Herder is right; suppose that fifth-century Greeks could aim only for an ideal quite different from that of the Babylonians; that the Egyptian view of life, because the people who held it lived in Egypt, which had a different geography and a different climate and so forth, and because the Egyptians have descended from people with a completely different ideology from that of the Greeks – that what the Egyptians wanted was different from what the Greeks wanted, but equally valid, equally fruitful – and Herder is one of those not very many thinkers in the world who really do absolutely adore things for being what they are, and do not condemn them for not being something else. For Herder everything is delightful. He is delighted by Babylon and he is delighted by Assyria, he is delighted by India and he is delighted by Egypt. He thinks well of the Greeks, he thinks well of the Middle Ages, he thinks well of the eighteenth century, he thinks well of almost everything except the immediate environment of his own time and place. If there is anything which Herder dislikes it is the elimination of one culture by another. He does not like Julius Caesar because Julius Caesar trampled on a lot of Asiatic cultures, and we shall now not know what the Cappadocians were really after. He does not like the Crusades, because the Crusades damaged the Byzantines, or the Arabs, and these cultures have every right to the richest and fullest self-expression, without the trampling feet of a lot of imperialist knights. He disliked every form of violence, coercion and the swallowing of one culture by another, because he wants everything to be what it is as much as it possibly can. Herder is the originator, the author, not of nationalism as is sometimes said, although no doubt some of his ideas entered nationalism, but of something – I do not quite know what name to give it – much more like populism. That is to say (to instance its more comical forms), he is the originator of all those antiquarians who want natives to remain as native as possible, who like arts and crafts, who detest standardisation – everyone who likes the quaint, people who wish to preserve the most exquisite forms of old provincialism without the impingement on it of some hideous metropolitan uniformity. Herder is the father, the ancestor, of all those travellers, all those amateurs, who go round the world ferreting out all kinds of forgotten forms of life, delighting in everything that is peculiar, everything that is odd, everything that is native, everything that is untouched. In that sense he did feed the streams of human sentimentality to a very high degree. At any rate, that is Herder's temperament and that is why, since he wants everything to be what it can be as much as possible, that is to say, develop itself to its richest and fullest extent, the notion that there can be one single ideal for all men, everywhere, becomes unintelligible. If the Greeks had an ideal which was perfect for them as Greeks; if the Romans had an ideal which was less perfect but was as much as could be done for people who were unfortunately Romans, who were obviously less gifted than the Greeks, at least from Herder's point of view; if the early Middle Ages produced magnificent works, in the form, say, of the Song of the Niebelungs (which he much admired) or the other early epics, which he regarded as the simple, heroic expressions of uncontaminated, fresh peoples still wandering in the woods, uncrushed by some fearful jealous neighbours, who trample upon their culture in a brutal way; if all this is true, we cannot have all these things together.

What is the ideal form of life? We cannot be both Greek and Phoenician and medieval, and Eastern and Western, and Northern and Southern. We cannot attain to the highest ideals of all the centuries and all the places at once. Since we cannot do that, the whole notion of the perfect life collapses – the whole notion of there being a human ideal which it is the business of all men to strive after, that there is some kind of answer to questions of this kind, even as there is an answer in chemistry or in physics or in mathematics to certain questions to which, in principle at least, some kind of final answer can be given; or if not a final answer, at any rate an answer which approximates to finality, which is more final than any we have obtained yet, with a hope, or at least a chance, that the further we proceed in the same direction the nearer to the final solution we come. If this is true of physics and of chemistry and of mathematics, and, as the eighteenth century thought, should be true of ethics, of politics, of aesthetics; if it is possible to lay down criteria which tell you what makes a perfect work of art, what makes a perfect life, what makes a perfect character, what makes a perfect political constitution; if it is possible to give these answers, they can be obtained only by supposing that all other answers, however interesting, however fascinating, are false. But if Herder is right; if it was right for the Greeks to proceed in the Greek direction, right for the Indians to proceed in an Indian direction; if the Greek ideal and the Indian ideal are totally incompatible, which he not merely confessed but emphasised with a kind of joy; if variety and difference are not merely a fact about the world but a splendid fact, which is what he thought it to be, arguing for the variety of the imagination of the creator and the splendour of human creative powers, and the infinite possibilities still before mankind, and the unfulfillability of human ambitions, and the general excitement of living in a world in which nothing can ever be fully exhausted – if that is the image, then the notion of a final answer to the question of how to live becomes absolutely meaningless. It can mean nothing at all, because all these answers are, presumably, incompatible with one another.

Hence Herder's final conclusion, namely that each human group must strive after that which lies in its bones, which is part of its tradition. Each man belongs to the group he belongs to; his business as a human being is to speak the truth as it appears to him; the truth as it appears to him is as valid as the truth as it appears to others. From this vast variety of colours a wonderful mosaic can be made, but nobody can see the whole mosaic, nobody can see all the trees, only God can see the entire universe. Men, because they belong where they belong, and live where they do, cannot. Each age has its own internal ideal, and therefore any form of nostalgic seeking after the past – for example, 'Why cannot we be like the Greeks? Why cannot we be like the Romans?', which is presumably what French political philosophers, or French painters, or French sculptors were saying to themselves in the eighteenth century – the whole notion of revival, the whole notion of going back to the Middle Ages, back to Roman virtues, back to Sparta, back to Athens, or alternatively any form of cosmopolitanism –

'Why cannot we create a world State of such a kind that everybody in it will fit smoothly like ideal bricks, will form a structure which will go on for ever and ever, because it is constructed upon an indestructible formula, which is *the* truth, obtained by infallible methods?' – all this must become nonsense, meaningless, self-contradictory; and by enabling this doctrine to emerge Herder did plunge a most terrible dagger into the body of European rationalism, from which it never recovered.

In this sense Herder is certainly one of the fathers of the romantic movement. That is to say, he is one of the fathers of the movement whose characteristic attributes include the denial of unity, the denial of harmony, the denial of the compatibility of ideals, whether in the sphere of action or in the sphere of thought. Lenz's postulate about action, which I quoted – action, always action, make room for action; we can live only in action, otherwise nothing is worth having – is very sympathetic to Herder's whole point of view, because for him life consists in expressing experience as it comes, communicating it to others with the whole of your undivided personality. As for what men will make of it in two hundred years' time, five hundred years' time, two thousand years' time, it does not matter, he does not care, he does not see why he should care. This is a very new and extremely revolutionary and upsetting note in what had for the last two thousand years been the solid *philosophia perennis* of the West, according to which all questions have true answers, all true answers are in principle discoverable, and all the answers are in principle compatible, or combinable into one harmonious whole like a jigsaw puzzle. If what Herder said was true, this view is false, and about this people then proceeded to argue and to struggle, both in practice and in theory, both in the course of national revolutionary wars and in the course of violent conflicts of doctrine and of practice, both in the arts and in thought, for the next hundred and seventy years.

4

THE RESTRAINED ROMANTICS

I TURN NOW to three German thinkers, two philosophers and one artist – a dramatist – who left a very profound imprint upon the entire romantic movement, both in Germany and beyond its borders. These romantics could justly be called 'restrained romantics'; thereafter I shall discuss the unrestrained romantics to whom this movement ultimately led.

'The nature of things', said Rousseau once, 'does not madden us, only ill will does.' This is probably true of the majority of mankind. But there were certain Germans in the eighteenth century of whom this is plainly false. They were maddened not merely by the ill will of persons but by the nature of things. One of these was the philosopher Immanuel Kant.

Kant hated romanticism. He detested every form of extravagance, fantasy, what he called *Schwärmerei*, any form of exaggeration, mysticism, vagueness, confusion. Nevertheless, he is justly regarded as one of the fathers of romanticism – in which there is a certain irony. He was brought up, like Hamann and like Herder, both of whom he knew, in a pietist atmosphere. He regarded Hamann as a pathetic and confused mystic, and he disliked Herder's writings for their vast generalisations unsupported by evidence, their enormous great imaginative sweeps, which he regarded as an offence against reason.

Kant was an admirer of the sciences. He had a precise and extremely lucid mind: he wrote obscurely but seldom imprecisely. He was a distinguished scientist himself (he was a cosmologist); he believed in scientific principles perhaps more deeply than in any others; he regarded it as his life's task to explain the foundations of scientific logic and scientific method. He disliked everything that was rhapsodical or confused in any respect. He liked logic and he liked rigour. He regarded those who objected to these qualities as simply mentally indolent. He said that logic and rigour were difficult exercises of the human mind, and that it was customary for those who found these things too difficult to invent objections of a different type. No doubt there is a great deal in what he said. But if he is in any respect the father of romanticism, it is not as a critic of the sciences, nor of course as a scientist himself, but specifically in his moral philosophy.

Kant was virtually intoxicated by the idea of human freedom. His pietist upbringing led not to rhapsodical self-communings, as it did in the case of Hamann and others, but to a kind of intense preoccupation with the inner, moral life of man. One of the propositions about which he was convinced was that every man as such is aware of the difference between, on the one hand, inclinations, desires, passions, which pull at him from outside, which are part of his emotional or sensitive or empirical nature; and on the other hand the notion of duty, of obligation to do what is right, which often came into conflict with desire for pleasure and with inclination. The confusion of the two appeared to him to be a primitive fallacy. He might well have quoted the famous words of Shaftesbury, who objected to the view of man as being determined or conditioned by outside factors. Man, said Shaftesbury at the beginning of the eighteenth century, is not 'a Tyger strongly chain'd', or 'a Monkey under the Discipline of the Whip' – that is to say, a tiger strongly chained by the fear of punishment, or a monkey under the influence of the whip of desire for reward, or, again, fear of punishment.

Man is free, man has original native liberty, and this liberty, according to Shaftesbury, gives us the privilege of our selves, and makes us our own. But this, in the case of Shaftesbury, was simply an *obiter dictum* which had not much to do with the rest of his philosophy. In the case of Kant it became an obsessive central principle. Man is man, for Kant, only because he chooses. The difference between man and the rest of nature, whether animal or inanimate or vegetable, is that other things are under the law of causality, other things follow rigorously some kind of foreordained schema of cause and effect, whereas man is free to choose what he wishes. This, the will, is the thing which distinguishes human beings from other objects in nature. The will is that which enables men to choose either good or evil, either right or wrong. There is no merit in choosing what is right unless it is possible to choose what is wrong. Creatures who are determined, by whatever causes, into perpetually choosing that which is good and beautiful and true could claim no merit for doing so, for however noble the results, the action would be automatic. Therefore Kant supposed that the whole notion of moral merit, the whole notion of moral desert, the whole notion which is entailed by the fact that we praise and we blame, that we consider that human beings are to be congratulated or condemned for acting in this or that way, presupposes the fact that they are able freely to choose. For this reason one of the things which he most strenuously disliked – in politics at any rate – was the notion of paternalism.

There are two main obstacles which obsessed Kant all his life. One is the obstruction of men, the other is the obstruction of things. The obstruction of men is a familiar enough theme. In a short essay called 'An Answer to the Question: "What is Enlightenment?" ' Kant lays it down that enlightenment is simply the ability of men to determine their own lives, the liberation of themselves from the leading-strings of others, the fact that men become mature and determine what to do, whether it be evil or whether it be good, without leaning excessively upon authority, upon governesses of one kind or another, upon the State, upon their parents, upon their nurses, upon tradition, upon any kind of established values on which the weight of moral responsibility is then squarely laid. A man is responsible for his own acts. If he gives this responsibility up, or if he is too immature to realise it, then he is *pro tanto* a barbarian, and not civilised – or a child. Civilisation is maturity, maturity is self-determination – being determined by rational considerations, and not being pushed and pulled about by something or other over which we have no control, in particular by other persons. 'A *paternalist government*', says Kant – and he is thinking about Frederick the Great, although it would no doubt have been unsafe for a professor in Königsberg to say so openly – based on the benevolence of a ruler who treats his subjects 'as un-grown-up children ... is the greatest conceivable *despotism*', and 'destroys all freedom'. And elsewhere he wrote: 'The man who stands in dependence on another is no longer a man at all, he has lost his standing, he is nothing but the possession of another man.'

Therefore Kant in his moral philosophy is particularly rabid against any form of domination of one human being by another. He is really the father of the notion of exploitation as an evil. I do not think you will find a very great deal before the late eighteenth century, and in particular before Kant, about exploitation as an evil. Indeed, why should it be regarded as so terrible that one man should use another man for his own purposes rather than this other man's? Perhaps there are worse vices, perhaps cruelty is worse, perhaps, as the Enlightenment maintained, ignorance is worse, or indolence, or other things of that sort. Not so for Kant. Any kind of use of other people for purposes which are not these other people's, but one's own, seems to him to be a form of degradation imposed by one man on another, some form of hideous maiming of other people, of removal from them of that which distinguishes them as men, namely their self-determining liberty. This is why you find in Kant such a passionate sermon against exploitation, degradation, dehumanisation, everything that afterwards becomes the stock-in-trade of all liberal and socialist writers in the nineteenth and twentieth centuries – the whole notion of degradation, reification, mechanisation of life, the alienation of human beings from one another or from their proper purposes, the use of men as things, the use of human beings as raw material for people to wreak their will on, the general view of human beings as entities which can be pushed about or determined or educated against their will. The monstrosity of that, the notion that this is morally the worst thing that one human being can do to another, stems from this passionate propaganda by Kant. No doubt it can be found in other authors, particularly Christian authors, before Kant, but it was he who secularised it and translated it into common European currency.

This is a very central notion indeed. Why did he feel this? Because he thought that values were entities which human beings generated themselves. The notion is this: If human beings depend for their actions on something outside themselves and outside their control, if in other words the source of their behaviour is not within them but in something else, then they cannot be regarded as responsible. If they are not responsible they are not fully moral beings. But if we are not moral beings, then our distinctions between right and wrong, free and unfree, duty and pleasure are delusions, and this he was not prepared to face, this he denied. He regarded it as a primary datum of human consciousness – at least as primary as the fact that we see tables and chairs and trees and objects in space, or that we have some kind of perception of other objects in nature – that we know that there are certain courses of action of which it can be said that we can either do them or refrain from doing them. This is a basic datum. If this is so, then it cannot be that values, namely aims or ends which human beings strive for, are outside us, whether in nature or in God, because if they were outside us, and if their intensity determined our actions, then we should be slaves to them – it would be an extremely sublime form of slavery, but slavery nevertheless. To be un-slavelike, to be free, is therefore to commit yourself freely to some kind of moral values. You can commit yourself to a value or not, but the liberty is in the commitment, not in the status, rational or otherwise, of the value itself; in the fact that you do or do not, can but need not, commit yourself to it. What you commit yourself to is another matter – that might be discoverable by rational means – but it is the commitment or the non-commitment alone that makes it a value for you. In other words, to call an act good or bad, to call it right or wrong, is in effect to say that there exist free self-committing acts – what later came to be called *engagé* behaviour, committed behaviour, un-indifferent behaviour – on the part of human beings.

This is what Kant means by saying that men are ends in themselves. What else could be an end? Men are choosers of acts. To sacrifice a man, you must sacrifice him to something higher than himself. But nothing is higher than that which is to be regarded as the highest moral value. But to call a thing a high moral value is to say that some man or other is prepared to live or die for it; unless somebody is prepared to live or die for it, there is no 'it' in the sense of a moral value. A value is made a value – at least a duty, a goal transcending desire and inclination, is so made – by human choice and not by some intrinsic quality in itself, out there. Values are not stars in some moral heaven, they are internal, they are what human beings freely choose to live for, to fight for, to die for. That is Kant's fundamental sermon. He does not offer a great deal of argument for it, he simply states it as a self-evident truth, in various types of propositions which more or less repeat each other.

But far more sinister, from Kant's point of view, even than the obstruction of men, or the enslavement of men, or men tampering with one another, or getting at one another, is the (for him) nightmare thought of determinism, of slavery at the hands of nature. If, says Kant in effect, that which is undoubtedly true about inanimate nature, namely the law of causality, were true about all aspects of human life, then indeed there would be no morality. For then men would be wholly conditioned by outside factors, and although they might deceive themselves into supposing that they were free, they would in fact be determined. In other words, for Kant determinism, particularly mechanical determinism, is incompatible with any freedom and any morality and must therefore be false. By determinism he means any kind of determination by outside factors, whether by the material factors – physical or chemical factors – about which the eighteenth century spoke, or by the passions, seen as irresistible to men. If you say about a passion, it is stronger than I, I could not help it, I yielded, I was pushed, I was unable, it overwhelmed me, you are in effect confessing to a certain kind of helplessness and slavery.

This need never be the case, for Kant. The free-will problem is an ancient conundrum; it was invented by the Stoics and it has troubled the human imagination and the human mind ever since. But Kant saw it as a kind of nightmarish dilemma; and when the official solution was produced for him, namely that while of course we choose as we choose (we can choose between one thing and another, nobody denies that), nevertheless the objects for us to choose between, and the fact that we are likely to choose in the way in which we do, are determined – in other words, when there are alternatives, though it is of course possible to do either one or the other, the fact that we are placed in a situation where *these* are the alternatives, and more than that, that our will is going to be determined in a certain direction, means that we do what we will, but our will itself is not free – that Kant called a miserable subterfuge which should not be able to take in anybody. Consequently he cut off all possible routes of escape – all the official routes which other philosophers, frightened by the same dilemma, had provided. This problem, although it was particularly acute for Kant, has dominated European thought, and indeed to some extent European action, ever since.

It is a problem which obsesses both philosophers and historians in the nineteenth century and, indeed, in our own century too. It is a problem which has come out with peculiar acuteness in various forms today, for example in the form of arguments between historians about the relative roles in history of individuals and vast impersonal forces, social or economic or psychological. It has come out in the form of various types of political theory: there are those who believe that men are determined, for example, by their objective position in a structure, say the class structure, and those who believe that men are not so determined, or at any rate not wholly so determined. It comes out in legal theory as a disagreement between people who think that crime is a disease and should be cured by medical means, because it is something for which the criminal is not responsible, and those who believe that the criminal can choose what to do, and therefore to cure him or to use medical treatment on him is an insult to his inborn human dignity. This was certainly the view taken by Kant. He believed in retributive punishment (which is today regarded as a retrograde point of view, and perhaps may indeed be so), because he thought that a man would prefer being sent to prison to going to a hospital; because he thought that if a man did something and was blamed for it, severely blamed or even punished, because he might have avoided it, this presupposed that he was a human being with the power of choice (even though he may have chosen what is evil), rather than treating him as conditioned by forces over which he had no control, say the unconscious, say the environment, say the treatment of him by his parents, or a thousand other factors which had rendered him incapable of acting otherwise – say ignorance, say physical disease of some kind. He thought that this was a deeper insult to him, inasmuch as it treated him as an animal or a thing rather than as a human being.

Kant is very passionate on this point, and I should like to bring out the full flavour of his views. For him generosity, for example, is a vice, because generosity is ultimately a form of condescension and patronage. It is ultimately what the 'haves' give to the 'have-nots'. In a world which was just, generosity would not be required. Pity appears to Kant to be a detestable quality. He would rather be ignored, he would rather be insulted, he would rather be badly treated than pitied, because pity entails a certain superiority on the part of the pitier for him who is pitied, and this superiority Kant stoutly denied. All men are equal, all men can determine themselves, and if one man pities another, he thereby reduces him to an animal or a thing, or at any rate to a pitiable or pitiful object, and this for Kant was a most fearful insult to human dignity and human morality.

That was Kant's moral view. What frightened him was the notion of the external world as a kind of treadmill, and if Spinoza and the determinists of the eighteenth century – for example Helvétius or Holbach or the scientists – are right; if, Kant declares, a man is simply an object in nature, simply a mass of flesh and bones and blood and nerves who is acted upon by external forces exactly as animals and objects are; then a man, as he says, is nothing but a 'turnspit'. He moves, but not through his own volition. Man is nothing but a clock. He is set, he ticks, but he does not set himself. This kind of freedom is no freedom at all, and has no moral value of any kind. Hence Kant's total denial of wholesale determinism, and his enormous emphasis upon the human will. This is what he calls autonomy; being pulled and pushed about by external factors, whether they be physical or emotional, he calls heteronomy, that is to say the laws the sources of which are outside the human being.

This entails a new and somewhat revolutionary view of nature, which again becomes an extremely central factor in European consciousness. Until then the attitude which was taken towards nature, whatever might be meant by that word – and some scholars have counted no fewer than two hundred meanings which are attached to the word 'nature' in the eighteenth century alone – was on the whole benevolent or respectful. Nature was regarded as a harmonious system, or at least a symmetrical, well-composed system, such that man suffered when he got out of gear with it.

Therefore the way to cure human beings when they were criminal or unhappy was somehow to restore them to what they should be, or to the bosom of nature. Although various views were taken of nature, as I explained earlier – mechanistic views, biological views, organic views, physical views (all kinds of metaphors are used) – there is always the same refrain: Mistress Nature, Dame Nature, nature's leading-strings, from which we ought not to detach ourselves. Even Hume, the least metaphysical of thinkers, believes that when men get out of sorts – if they become unhappy or mad – nature usually asserts herself; this means that certain fixed habits assert themselves and a healing process occurs, the wound heals, and men are reintegrated into the harmonious flow or system, depending on whether you regard nature as static or as a moving affair; anyhow, men are restored by being somehow reabsorbed into this large and comforting medium which man should never have deserted.

For Kant this plainly cannot be true. The notion of Mistress Nature, Dame Nature, something benevolent, something you worshipped, something which art ought to imitate, something which morals ought to derive from, something which politics are founded upon, as Montesquieu said – this derogates from man's inborn liberty of choice, because nature is mechanical, or even if not mechanical, even if it is organic, at any rate every event in nature follows by a rigorous necessity from every other; and therefore, if man is part of nature, then he is determined, and morality is a hideous illusion. Therefore nature in Kant becomes at worst an enemy, at best simply neutral stuff which one moulds. Man is conceived of as in part a natural object: plainly his body is in nature; his emotions are in nature; all the various things which are capable of making him heteronomous, or depend upon something other than his true self, are natural; but when he is at his freest, when he is at his most human, when he rises to his noblest heights, then he dominates nature, that is to say he moulds her, he breaks her, he imposes his personality upon her, he does that which he chooses, because he commits himself to certain ideals; and by committing himself to these ideals he imposes his seal upon nature, and nature therefore becomes plastic stuff. Some bits of nature are more plastic than others, but all nature must be presented to man as something with which or upon which or at which he does something, not something to which he – not the whole of him, at any rate – belongs.

This notion that nature is an enemy or neutral stuff is something relatively new. That is why Kant acclaimed the French constitution of 1790. Here at last, he said, was a form of government in which all men, at least theoretically, were able to vote freely, to speak their views; they need no longer obey a government, no matter how benevolent, no longer obey a Church, no matter how excellent, no longer obey principles, no matter how ancient, provided they were not of their own making. Once man was encouraged, as he was by the French constitution, to vote freely in accordance with his own inner decision – not impulse, Kant would not have called it that – his own inner will, he was thereby liberated, and, whether Kant interpreted it correctly or incorrectly, it appeared to him that the French Revolution was a great liberating act, inasmuch as it asserted the value of individual souls. He said much the same about the American Revolution too. When his colleagues deplored the Terror, and regarded all the events in France with undisguised horror, Kant, although he did not exactly openly approve, never quite retreated from his position that it was at any rate an experiment in the right direction, even if it went wrong. This indicates the passion with which this normally very conventional, very obedient, very tidy, old-fashioned, somewhat provincial East Prussian professor nevertheless regarded this great liberating chapter in the history of the human race, the self-assertion of human beings against huge idols, as he thought of them, standing over against them. Tradition, unbreakable ancient principles, kings, governments, parents, all kinds of authority accepted simply because it is authority – all this revolted him. He is not normally thought of in these terms, but there is no doubt that his moral philosophy is firmly founded upon this anti-authoritarian principle.

This, of course, was to assert the primacy of the will. In a certain sense Kant was still a child of eighteenth-century enlightenment, because he thought that all men, if their hearts were pure, and when they asked themselves what it was right to do, would in similar circumstances arrive at identical conclusions, because to all questions reason must in all men give the selfsame answer. This was also believed by Rousseau. Kant at one time believed that only a minority of human beings were enlightened enough, or experienced enough, or morally lofty enough to be able to give the correct answers. Under the impulse of reading Rousseau's *Émile*, which he admired very greatly – indeed, a picture of Rousseau was the only human representation to be found above Kant's desk – he came to believe that all men were capable of this. Any man, whatever else he might lack – he might be ignorant, he might know no chemistry, he might know no logic, he might know no history – was capable of discovering rational answers to the question: How shall I behave? And all rational answers to it must of necessity coincide.[1] I repeat: a man who simply acts from impulse, however generous, a man who acts from his natural character, however noble, a man who acts under any kind of ineluctable pressure, whether it be from outside or from his own inner nature, is not acting, at least not a moral agent. The only thing worth possessing is the unfettered will – this is the central proposition which Kant put on the map. And it was destined to have exceedingly revolutionary and subversive consequences, which he could hardly have anticipated.

All kinds of versions of this doctrine appear towards the end of the eighteenth century, but perhaps the most vivid and the most interesting from our point of view is that of his faithful disciple, the dramatist, poet and historian Friedrich Schiller. Schiller is as intoxicated by the idea of will, liberty, autonomy, man on his own as Kant was. Unlike previous thinkers, unlike Helvétius, unlike Holbach, who simply believed that there were certain correct answers to social questions, and to moral and artistic and economic questions, and to factual questions of every kind, and that the important thing was simply to get human beings to understand these answers and to act accordingly – how you got them to do this mattered relatively little – in strict opposition to this, Schiller is constantly harping upon the fact that the only thing which makes

[1] As to the fallacies of this doctrine, I shall not enter into them here, for it would take me too far afield; but this is the only thin cord by which Kant is still bound to eighteenth-century rationalism.

man man is the fact that he is able to rise above nature and mould her, crush her, subjugate her to his beautiful, unfettered, morally directed will.

There are certain characteristic expressions which Schiller uses throughout his writings, not only in his philosophical essays, but also in his plays. He constantly speaks of spiritual freedom: freedom of reason, the kingdom of freedom, our free self, inner freedom, freedom of mind, moral freedom, the free intelligence – a very favourite phrase – holy freedom, the impregnable citadel of freedom; and there are expressions in which instead of the word 'freedom' he uses the word 'independence'. Schiller's theory of tragedy is founded upon this notion of freedom; his practice as a tragic writer and his poetry are impregnated with this notion; and that is the way in which, perhaps more than through direct reading of Kant, it had such a powerful effect upon romantic art, both poetical and plastic. Tragedy does not consist in the mere spectacle of suffering: if man were pure mind he would not suffer at all. Helpless suffering, suffering which man cannot avoid, a man crushed by misfortune, is not an object of tragedy. It is merely an object of horror, pity, and perhaps disgust. The only thing which can be regarded as properly tragic is resistance, resistance on the part of a man to whatever it is that oppresses him. Laocoon, who resists his natural impulse to escape, not to behave in accordance with the truth as he knows it; Regulus, who surrendered himself to the Carthaginians, although no doubt he might have lived a more comfortable and perhaps not less disgraceful life if he had remained in Rome; Milton's Satan, who, after he has seen the appalling spectacle of Hell, nevertheless continues with his evil designs – these are tragic figures because they assert themselves, because they are not tempted into conformity, because they do not yield to temptation, whether it takes the form of pleasure or of pain, whether physical temptation or moral temptation, because they cross their arms upon the crossroads, and they defy nature; and defiance – moral defiance in Schiller's case; not any defiance, but defiance in the name of some ideal to which you seriously commit yourself – is what makes for tragedy, because it creates a conflict, a conflict in which man is grappling against forces either too great for him or not, as the case may be.

Richard III, Iago are not tragic figures for Schiller, because they behave like animals, they behave under the impulse of passion; therefore, he says, since we are not thinking about human beings, since we are not thinking in moral terms, we watch with fascination the marvellously ingenious behaviour of these intriguing human animals, who do behave in the most remarkable fashion: Shakespeare's genius and fantasy make them go through extraordinary convolutions in some respects intellectually superior to those of the average man. But as soon as you think of what is happening you realise that they are behaving under the influence of passion, which they cannot avoid. Once this is seen they are no longer human beings for us and we are ashamed and disgusted. We think that because they are not behaving as human beings, because they have resigned their humanity, they are therefore detestable and dehumanised, and therefore not tragic figures. Nor, I regret to say, is Lovelace in Richardson's novel *Clarissa*: he is simply an amorist who pursues various ladies under the impulse of ungovernable passion; if it is truly ungovernable, there is no tragedy, whatever may occur.

Schiller thinks that drama perhaps acts as a kind of inoculation. If we ourselves were in the situation of Laocoon, or in the situation of Oedipus or whoever it may be, struggling against fate, we might succumb. Also the terror of being in such a situation might be so great that our feelings would be numbed, or we should be driven out of our minds. We cannot tell how we should behave; but by watching these things on the stage we remain relatively cool and detached, and therefore the experience performs an educational and persuasive function. We observe what it is for a man to behave like a man, and the purpose of art, the purpose at least of dramatic art, which is concerned with human beings, is to show human beings behaving in the manner which is most human. That is Schiller's doctrine; and it derives directly from Kant.

Nature herself is indifferent to man, nature herself is amoral, nature herself destroys us in the most ruthless and hideous fashion, and this is what makes us particularly aware of the fact that we are not part of her. Let me quote a typical passage from Schiller:

The very circumstance that nature, regarded as a whole, mocks all the rules that our understanding prescribes for her, that she proceeds on her free and capricious career and treads in the dust the creations of wisdom without regard for them, that she snatches up what is significant and what is trivial, what is noble and what is common, and involves them in a hideous identical disaster, that she preserves the world of ants and seizes man, her most glorious creature, in her giant's arms and crushes him, that she often dissipates man's most arduous achievements and indeed her own most arduous achievements in one frivolous hour and devotes centuries to work of unnecessary folly . . .

This Schiller regards as typical of nature, and it underlines and emphasises and brings out the fact that this is nature and not art, this is nature and not man, this is nature and not morality. And so he makes a vast contrast between nature, which is this elemental, capricious, perhaps causal, perhaps chance-directed entity, and man, who has morality, who distinguishes between desire and will, duty and interest, the right and the wrong, and acts accordingly, if need be against nature.

That is the central doctrine in Schiller, and it emerges in most of his tragedies. Let me give a very typical example, which will show to what lengths he went. Schiller rejected the Kantian solution, fundamentally because it seemed to him that though Kant's will liberates us from nature, he puts us on a very narrow moral road, into too grim, too confining a Calvinist world, where the only alternatives are either being the plaything of nature or following this grim path of Lutheran duty which Kant thought in terms of – a path which maims and destroys, cramps and crimps human nature. If man is to be free he must be free not merely to do his duty, he must be free to choose between either following nature or doing his duty quite freely. He must stand above both duty and nature and be able to choose either. In discussing Corneille's *Medea*, Schiller makes this point. In Corneille's play Medea, princess of Colchis, because she becomes angry with Jason, who first abducts her from Colchis, and then abandons her, proceeds to kill her own children – in fact she boils them alive. Schiller does not approve of this action, but he says that Medea is nevertheless heroic and Jason is not. Because Medea defies nature, defies nature in herself, defies her maternal instinct, defies her own affection for her children, she rises above nature and acts freely; what she does

81

may be abominable, but in principle she is somebody who is capable of reaching loftier heights, because she is free and not under the impulsion of nature, than poor philistine Jason, who is a perfectly decent Athenian of his time and generation and who lives a perfectly ordinary life, not entirely blameless but not tragically sinister either, and who simply drifts along with the tide of conventional sentiment – and that is perfectly worthless. Medea at least is somebody, and could easily have attained heights of moral grandeur: Jason is nobody.

This is the kind of category which he uses in his other plays as well. In *Fiesco*, one of his early plays, the eponymous hero is the tyrant of Genoa, and no doubt he does wrong; he oppresses the Genoese. Still, although he does what is bad, he is superior to the knaves and the fools, the ignoramuses and the rabble of Genoa, who need a master, and whom he therefore dominates; and no doubt it may be right for the republican leader Verrina to drown him, as finally he does in the play; nevertheless we lose something in Fiesco. He is as a human being qualitatively superior to the persons who correctly murder him. This, roughly speaking, is Schiller's doctrine, and it is the beginning of that famous doctrine of the great sinner and the superfluous man which was destined to play a part in nineteenth-century art.

Werther died quite uselessly. René in Chateaubriand's story of the same name dies quite uselessly. They die uselessly because they belong to a society which is incapable of making use of them; they are superfluous persons; they are superfluous because their morality, which is a morality superior, we are meant to understand, to that of the society around them, has no opportunity of asserting itself against the fearful opposition offered by the philistines, the slaves, the heteronomous creatures of the society in which they live. This is the beginning of a long line of superfluous men, particularly celebrated in Russian literature, of Griboedov's Chatsky, of Evgeny Onegin, of Turgenev's superfluous persons, of Oblomov – of all the various characters who occur in the Russian novel up to and including *Dr Zhivago*. This is the origin of this tradition.

There is also the other line, the men who say that if society is bad, if it is impossible to obtain the proper morality, if everything one does is obstructed, if there is nothing to be done, then down with the society – let it be ruined, let it go – all crime is permitted. This is the beginning of the great sinner in Dostoevsky, the Nietzschean figure who wishes to raze to the ground a society whose system of values is such that a superior person who truly understands what it is to be free cannot operate in terms of it, and therefore prefers to destroy it, prefers indeed to destroy the principles in terms of which he himself sometimes acts, prefers self-destruction, suicide, to continuing to drift along simply as an object in an uncontrollable stream. This originates with Schiller, under the influence, oddly enough, of Kant, who would have been horrified to perceive any such consequences of his perfectly orthodox, half-pietist, half-Stoical doctrine.

This is one of the great motifs in the romantic movement, and if we ask when, chronologically, it occurs, it is not always altogether difficult to identify it. Towards the end of the 1760s Lessing wrote a play called *Minna von Barnhelm*. I shall not attempt to summarise the plot of this not altogether interesting play beyond simply saying that the hero of it is a man called Major Tellheim, a man of honour who is badly treated – injustice is done to him – and who, because he has a very acute sense of his own honour, refuses to meet the lady whom he loves and who loves him. He supposes that she may suppose that he has performed an act which is not altogether honourable, although he is in fact quite innocent; and because she may think it, therefore it is impossible for him to face her until and unless it has been made quite clear that in fact he is innocent, and in fact does not deserve any possible negative attitude which a conceivable misunderstanding of his action might entail. He behaves very honourably but rather foolishly. Lessing's point is that although he was a good man, indeed a nice man, nevertheless he is not a very sensible man – rather like Molière's not dissimilar misanthrope – and in the end the play ends quite happily because the lady turns out to be a great deal more sensible (like Alceste's friend in Molière) than the gentleman, and manages to create a situation in which his innocence is triumphantly displayed, and they are united and are happy for ever, we are meant to understand. She is the heroine; she speaks for the author with

83

her good sense, toleration, maturity, her humane and compassionate sense of reality. Tellheim is a man who is wronged by society, who passionately pursues certain ideals of his own – honour, integrity in an extreme form – who is thoroughly *engagé* and committed, who is in fact everything that Schiller wants people to be.

In the early 1780s Schiller wrote *The Robbers*, the play whose hero, as I have said, is Karl Moor, who has also been wronged, and who because he has been wronged becomes the head of a robber gang, and murders and pillages and sets buildings on fire, and in the end surrenders himself to justice and causes himself to be executed. Karl Moor is the same Major Tellheim promoted to heroic status. Therefore if we wish to know the moment that the romantic hero genuinely emerges, he emerges – at least in Germany, which seems to me to be the motherland of this figure – somewhere between the end of the 1760s and the beginning of the 1780s, for what sociological reasons I shall not attempt to explain.

In Molière's *Le Misanthrope*, for example, Alceste is somebody who is bitterly disappointed by the world, who cannot abide, cannot adjust himself to, its false and trivial and repulsive values, but he is not the hero of the play. There are more sensible persons in the play who ultimately try to bring him to his senses, and do so. He is not detestable, he is not contemptible, but he is not the hero. He is, if anything, comical; so is Tellheim faintly comical – disarming, agreeable, amiable, morally attractive, but faintly ridiculous. By 1780 such a figure is not faintly ridiculous, he is satanic, and this is the change, this is the great break between what might be called the rationalist or the enlightened tradition, or the tradition that there is a nature of things which must be learnt, which must be understood, which must be known, and to which people must adjust themselves at the cost of either destroying or making fools of themselves – between that tradition and the tradition where, on the contrary, man commits himself to the values to which he commits himself, and, if need be, perishes in their defence heroically. In other words the notion of martyrdom, heroism, as a quality to be worshipped for its own sake, seems to emerge about then.

Schiller's fundamental view is that man goes through three

stages: first what he calls the *Notstaat*, that is to say the state which is governed by necessity, in the form of something called the *Stofftrieb* – 'stuff-drive' is the literal translation, 'drive' in the modern psychological sense. In this stage, that is, man is driven by the nature of matter. This is a kind of Hobbesian jungle in which human beings are possessed by passions and by desires, in which they have no ideals, in which they simply collide with each other, and where it is necessary somehow to separate them from each other. This is a state which Schiller calls savage. It is followed by a state which is not savage, but in which, on the contrary, men, in order to improve their condition, adopt very rigid principles, and make these principles a kind of fetish; and this Schiller calls a barbarian state, interestingly enough. A savage for him is somebody driven by passions which he cannot master. Barbarians are people who worship idols, for example absolute principles, without quite knowing why – because they are taboos, because they are laid down, because they are a decalogue, because somebody told them they were absolute, because they proceed from a source of dark and unquestionable authority. That is what he calls barbarism. Because these taboos come to claim rational authority, this second state is called the *Vernunftstaat*, the rational state – Kant and his commandments.

But this is not enough, and there is a third condition, towards which Schiller aspires. Like all idealist writers of his time, Schiller imagines that once upon a time there was a marvellous human unity, a golden age, where passion was not divided from reason, and liberty was not divided from necessity. Then something appalling happened: division of labour, inequality, civilisation – in short, culture occurred, rather on the lines of Rousseau, and, as a result of this, ungovernable desires, jealousies, envies, men divided against other men, men divided against themselves, fraud, misery, alienation. How are we to get back to this original state without lapsing into some kind of innocence or childishness which is plainly neither feasible nor desirable? This must be done, according to Schiller, by means of art, liberation by art. What does he have in mind?

Schiller speaks about the *Spieltrieb*, 'play-drive'. He says that the only way in which human beings can liberate themselves is by adopting the attitude of games-players. What does he mean? Art for him is a form of play, and he explains that the difficulty for him is to reconcile on the one hand the necessities of nature, which cannot be avoided, and which cause stress, and on the other hand these rigorous commandments which narrow and contract life. The only way to do that is by placing ourselves in the position of people who freely imagine and freely invent. If we are children at play – to take the very simplest instance, although it is not Schiller's – we can impersonate Red Indians, and if we imagine ourselves to be Red Indians, we are for these purposes Red Indians, and we obey the rules of Red Indians, without a sense of pressure; there is no pressure upon us because we invent the rules, and our parts, ourselves. Anything we make is ours, anything we make does not constrict us. Therefore if only we can transform ourselves into creatures who obey laws not because these laws are made for us by others, not because we are terrified of them, not simply because they are laid down by some frowning deity, or by terrifying men, or by Kant, or by nature herself; if we can only obey these laws because we choose to do so freely, because this expresses the ideal human life as we, who have learnt from history and the wisdom of thinkers, see it, exactly as people who play invent their game and then obey its laws with enthusiasm, with passion, with pleasure, because this is a work of art which they themselves have constructed; if only we can do that, in other words if only we can convert the necessity of obeying rules into some kind of almost instinctive, perfectly free, harmonious, spontaneous, natural operation; if we can only do that, we are saved.

How are men to be reconciled to each other? Human beings might play very different games, and these games could easily involve them in disasters as great as any others. Schiller goes back, not very effectively or convincingly, to the Kantian principle that if we are rational, if we are like the Greeks, if we are harmonious, if we understand ourselves, if we understand what freedom is, if we understand what morality is, if we understand what the pleasures and the heavenly delight of artistic creation is, then surely we shall somehow achieve a harmonious relation with other creators, other artists equally concerned not with mowing other men down, not with crushing them, but with living with them in some happy, united, creative world. This is the kind of Utopia in which Schiller's thought, more or less, ends. It is not very convincing, but its general direction is fairly clear, that is, that artists are people who obey rules of their own making; they invent the rules, and they invent the objects they create. The material may be given by nature, but everything else is made by them.

This introduces for the first time what seems to me to be a crucial note in the history of human thought, namely that ideals, ends, objectives are not to be discovered by intuition, by scientific means, by reading sacred texts, by listening to experts or to authoritative persons; that ideals are not to be discovered at all, they are to be invented; not to be found but to be generated, generated as art is generated. Birds, says Schiller, inspire us, because we think, however falsely, that they dominate gravity, they fly, rise above necessity, which we cannot do. A vase inspires us because it is a triumph over brute matter, a triumph if you like of form, but of freely invented form, not of those rigorous forms which Calvinists and Lutherans and other religions or other secular tyrannies have imposed. Hence the passion for invented forms, ideals which men make. Once upon a time we were integral, we were Greeks. (This is the great myth of the Greeks, which is historically no doubt quite absurd, but dominated the Germans in their political helplessness – Schiller and Hölderlin and Hegel and Schlegel and Marx.) We were children playing in the sunlight, we did not distinguish between necessity and freedom, between passion and reason, and this was a happy and innocent time. But this time is past, innocence is gone; life no longer offers us these things; what we are now offered as a description of the universe is nothing but a grim causal treadmill; we must therefore reassert our humanity, invent our own ideals, and these ideals, because they are invented, are in opposition to nature, not part of her but directed against her; therefore idealism – the invention of ends – is a break with nature, and our task is so to transform nature, so to educate ourselves, as to make our own given, not too flexible, nature permit us to follow and to realise an ideal in some beautiful and frictionless manner.

There he leaves it. That is the heritage of Schiller, which afterwards entered very deeply into the souls of the romantics, who abandoned the notion of harmony, who abandoned the notion of reason, and who became, as I said earlier, somewhat more unbridled.

The third thinker about whom I must say a word is Fichte, who was a philosopher and a disciple of Kant, and who also added to this notion of freedom a particularly passionate exposition of it, as a typical quotation illustrates. 'At the mere mention of the name freedom', says Fichte, 'my heart opens and flowers, while at the word necessity it contracts painfully.' This shows the kind of person he was temperamentally, and indeed he himself said: 'A man's philosophy is as his nature, not his nature as his philosophy.' Hegel spoke about Fichte's tendency to feel gloom, horror, abhorrence at the mere thought of the eternal laws of nature and their strict necessity. There are people who are temperamentally depressed by the thought of this rigid order, this unbreakable symmetry, the inescapable kind of world in which everything follows everything else in some ineluctable, orderly, totally unalterable way; and Fichte was among these.

Fichte's contribution to romantic thought consists in this. He says: if you are simply a contemplative being and ask for the answers to questions such as what to do, or how to live in the realm of knowledge, you will never discover an answer. You will never discover an answer simply because knowledge always presupposes some larger knowledge: you arrive at a proposition and you ask for the authority for it, and then some other knowledge, some other proposition, is brought in in order to validate the first one. Then that proposition in turn needs validation, some wider generalisation is needed for the purpose of bolstering up that idea, and so on *ad infinitum*. Therefore there is no end to this search, and we simply end up with a Spinozist system, which at best is simply a rigid, logical unity in which there is no room for movement.

This is not true, says Fichte. Our lives do not depend upon contemplative knowledge. Life does not begin with disinterested contemplation of nature or of objects. Life begins with action. Knowledge is an instrument, as afterwards William James and Bergson and many others were to repeat; knowledge is simply an instrument provided by nature for the purpose of effective life, of action; knowledge is knowing how to survive, knowing what to do, knowing how to be, knowing how to adapt things to our use, knowing, in other words, how to live (and what to do in order not to perish), in some unawakened, semi-instinctive fashion. This knowledge, which is the acceptance of certain things in the world, willy-nilly because we cannot help it, because it is presupposed in the biological urge, in the necessity of living, is for Fichte a kind of act of faith. 'We do not act because we know,' he says, 'we know because we are called upon to act.' Knowledge is not a passive state. External nature impinges upon us, and stops us, but it is clay for our creation; if we create we have freedom again. Then he makes an important proposition: Things are as they are, not because they are so independent of me, but because I make them so; things depend upon the way in which I treat them, what I need them for. This is a kind of early but extremely far-reaching pragmatism. Food is not what I hunger for, it is made food by my hunger, he says. 'I do not hunger for food because it is laid beside me; because I hunger, the object becomes food.' 'I do not accept what nature offers because I must': that is what animals do. I do not simply register what occurs like a kind of machine – that is what Locke and Descartes said human beings do, but this is false. 'I do not accept what nature offers because I must, I believe it because I will.'

Who is master, nature or I? 'I am not determined by ends, ends are determined by me.' 'The world', in the words of a commentator, 'is the poem thus dreamed out by the inner life.' This is a very dramatic, very poetical way of saying that experience is something which I determine because I act. Because I live in a certain way, things appear to me in a certain fashion: the world of a composer is different from the world of a butcher; the world of a man in the seventeenth century is different from the world of a man in the twelfth century. There may be certain things which are common, but there are more things, or more important things at any rate, which, for him, are not. So Schlegel said: Robbers are romantic because I make them romantic; nothing is romantic by nature. Freedom is action, not some contemplative state. 'To be free', says Fichte, 'is nothing, to become free is very heaven.' I make my world as I make a poem. Yet freedom is double-edged: because I am free I am able to exterminate others; freedom is freedom to commit evil acts. Savages kill each other, and civilised nations, says Fichte, with a certain prescience, using the power of law, of unity and of culture, will go on exterminating each other. Culture is not a deterrent to violence. This was a statement which the whole eighteenth century would almost unitedly (though there are exceptions) have rejected. For the eighteenth century, culture was a deterrent to violence because culture was knowledge, and knowledge proved the inadvisability of violence.[1] This was not so for Fichte: the only deterrent to violence is not culture, but some kind of moral regeneration – 'Man should be and do something.'

Fichte's whole notion is that man is a kind of continuous action – not even an actor. In order to rise to his full height he must constantly go on generating and creating. A man who does not create, a man who simply accepts what life or nature offers him, is dead. This is true not only of human beings, but also of nations (I will not here go into the political implications of Fichte's doctrine). Fichte began by talking about individuals, then he asked himself what an individual was, how one could become a perfectly free individual. One obviously cannot become perfectly free so long as one is a three-dimensional object in space, because nature confines one in a thousand ways. Therefore the only perfectly free being is something larger than man, it is something internal – although I cannot force my body, I can force my spirit. Spirit for Fichte is not the spirit of an individual man, but something which is common to many men, and it is common to many men because each individual spirit is imperfect, because it is to some extent hemmed in and confined by the particular body which it inhabits. But if you ask what pure spirit is, pure spirit is some kind of transcendent entity (rather like God), a central fire of which we are all individual sparks – a mystical notion which goes back at least to Boehme.

Gradually, after Napoleon's invasions and the general rise of nationalist sentiment in Germany, Fichte began thinking that perhaps what Herder said of human beings was true, that a man was made a man by other men, that a man was made a man by education, by language. Language was not invented by me, it was

[1] This was rejected by the Scottish writer Ferguson – and perhaps by Burke – but by whom else?

invented by others, and I am part of some common stream in which I am an element. My traditions, my customs, my outlook, everything about me is to some extent a creation of other men with whom I form an organic unity. So, gradually, he moved from the notion of the individual as an empirical human being in space to the notion of the individual as something larger, say a nation, say a class, say a sect. Once you move to that, then it becomes *its* business to act, it becomes *its* business to be free, and for a nation to be free means to be free of other nations, and if other nations obstruct it, it must make war.

So Fichte ends as a rabid German patriot and nationalist. If we are a free nation, if we are a great creator engaged upon creating those great values which in fact history has imposed upon us, because we happen not to have been corrupted by the great decadence which has fallen upon the Latin nations; if we happen to be younger, healthier, more vigorous than those decadent peoples (and here Francophobia emerges again) who are nothing but the debris of what was once no doubt a fine Roman civilisation – if that is what we are, then we must be free at the expense of no matter what, and therefore, since the world cannot be half slave and half free, we must conquer the others, and absorb them into our texture. To be free is to be free of obstacles, to be free is to make free with, to be free is to be able not to be obstructed by anything in the full exercise of your enormous creative drive. So we get the beginnings of this notion of vast nationalist or class-inspired collective drives forward, a mystical notion of men creatively lunging forward for the purpose of not being frozen, not being dead, not being oppressed by anything which is static, whether it be static nature, whether it be institutions, moral principles, political principles, artistic principles or anything else which is not made by them and which is not in process of constant fluid transformation. This is the beginning of the vast drive forward on the part of inspired individuals, or inspired nations, constantly creating themselves afresh, constantly aspiring to purify them-selves, and to reach some unheard-of height of endless self-transformation, endless self-creation, works of art constantly engaged in creating themselves, forward, forward, like a kind of vast cosmic design perpetually renewing itself. This half-metaphysical, half-religious notion, which emerges from the sober pages of Kant, and which Kant repudiated with the greatest possible vehemence and indignation, was destined to have an extremely violent effect upon both German politics and German morals, but also upon German art, German prose and German verse, and then by natural transference upon the French, and upon the English as well.

5

UNBRIDLED ROMANTICISM

I NOW COME to the final eruption of unbridled romanticism. According to Friedrich Schlegel, who wrote most authoritatively about this movement, and was indeed a part of it himself, the three factors which most profoundly influenced the entire movement, not only aesthetically but also morally and politically, were, in this order, Fichte's theory of knowledge, the French Revolution, and Goethe's famous novel *Wilhelm Meister*. This is probably a just attribution, and I should like to make it clear why this was so, and in what sense.

In my remarks about Fichte I spoke about his glorification of the active, dynamic and imaginative self. The innovation which Fichte brought into both theoretical philosophy and the theory of art – and to some extent of life – was roughly this. He accepted the view of the empiricists of the eighteenth century that there was some problem about what was meant by speaking about oneself. Hume had said that when he looked within himself as people normally do, when he introspected, he discovered a great many sensations, emotions, fragments of memory, of hope and fear – all kinds of small psychological units – but he failed to perceive any entity which could justly be called a self, and therefore concluded that the self was not a thing, not an object of direct perception, but perhaps simply a name for the concatenation of experiences out of which human personality and human history were formed, simply a kind of string which held together the onions, except that there was no string.

This proposition was accepted by Kant, who then made valiant efforts to recapture some kind of self, but much more passionately by the German romantics, in particular by Fichte, who laid down the doctrine that it was quite natural that the self should not emerge in cognition. When you are wholly absorbed in an object, whether in looking at a material object in nature, or in listening to sounds – music or something else – or in any other kind of process in which there is an object before you in the contemplation of which you are wholly absorbed, then naturally you are *pro tanto* not aware of yourself as the absorber. You become aware of the self only when there is some kind of resistance. You become aware of yourself not as an object but as that which is obtruded upon by some kind of recalcitrant reality. When you are looking at something and something intervenes, when you are listening to something and there is some kind of obstacle, it is the impact of the obstacle upon you which makes you aware of your self as an entity different from the not-self which you are trying to understand, or to feel, or perhaps to dominate, conquer, alter, mould – at any rate do something to or at. Therefore the Fichtean doctrine, which then becomes the authorised doctrine not only of the romantic movement, but of a great deal of psychology besides, is that the 'I', the 'self' in that sense of the word, is not the same as 'me'. 'Me' is something which no doubt can be introspected, which psychologists talk about, which scientific treatises can be written about, an object of some kind of inspection, an object of study, an object of psychology, sociology and the like. But there is a kind of non-accusative 'I', the primal nominative, which you become aware of, not at all in the act of cognition, but simply through being impacted upon. This Fichte called the *Anstoß*, 'impact', and it appeared to him to be the fundamental category which dominated all experience. That is to say, when you asked yourself what reason you had for supposing that the world existed, what reason you had for supposing you were not deluded, what reason you had for supposing that solipsism was not true, and that everything was not a figment of your imagination, or in some other way wholly delusive and deceiving, the answer was that you could not doubt that some kind of clash or collision occurred between you and what you wanted, between you and what you wished to be, between you and the stuff upon which you wished to impose your personality and which, *pro tanto*, resisted. In the resistance emerged the self and the not-self. Without the not-self, no sense of the self. Without the sense of the self, no sense of the not-self. This was a primary datum more radical, more basic, than anything which later supervened upon it or could be deduced from it. The world as described by the sciences was an artificial construction in relation to this absolutely primary, irreducible, fundamental datum, not even of experience, but of being. This, roughly, is Fichte's doctrine.

From this he expands the whole vast vision which then proceeds to dominate the imaginations of the romantics, whereby the only thing which is worthwhile, as I have tried to explain, is the exfoliation of a particular self, its creative activity, its imposition of forms upon matter, its penetration of other things, its creation of values, its dedication of itself to these values. This can have its political implications, as I hinted, if the self is no longer identified with the individual but with some super-personal entity, such as a community or a Church or a State or a class, which then becomes a huge intrusive forward-marching will, which imposes its particular personality both upon the outside world and upon its own constituent elements, which might be human beings, who are thereby reduced to the role simply of ingredients of, or parts in, some much bigger, much more impressive, much more historically persistent personality.

Let me quote a passage from Fichte's famous speeches to the German nation, delivered when Napoleon had conquered Prussia. These speeches were delivered to not very many people and had no great impact when they were delivered. Nevertheless, when they were read afterwards they produced a vast nationalist upsurge of feeling, and went on being read by Germans throughout the nineteenth century, and became their Bible after 1918. I need only quote a few lines out of this little book of lectures to indicate the kind of tone in question – the kind of propaganda which Fichte was at this period engaged in making. He says:

Either you believe in an original principle in man – a freedom, a perfectibility, an infinite progress of our species – or you believe in none of this. You may even have a feeling or some kind of intuition of its opposite. All those who have within them the creative quickening of life, or else, assuming that such a gift has been withheld from them, at least await the moment when they are caught up in the magnificent torrent of flowing and original life, or perhaps have some confused presentiment of such freedom, and have towards this phenomenon not hatred, nor fear, but a feeling of love, these are part of primal humanity. These may be considered as a true people, these constitute the *Urvolk*, the primal people – I mean the Germans. All those, on the other hand, who have resigned themselves to represent only the derivative, the second-hand product, who think of themselves in this way, become such an effect, and shall pay the price of their belief. They are a mere annexe to life. Not for them those pure springs which flowed before them and which still may be flowing around them. They are but an echo coming from a distant rock, from a voice which is now silent. They are excluded from the *Urvolk*, they are strangers, they are outsiders. The nation which bears the name 'German' to this day has not ceased to give evidence of a creative and original activity in the most diverse fields.

He then goes on:

And this is the principle of exclusion that I adopt. All those who believe in spiritual reality, those who believe in the freedom of the life of the spirit, those who believe in the eternal progress of the spirit through the instrumentality of freedom, whatever be their native land, whatever the language which they speak, they are our race, they are part of our people, or they will join it late or soon. All those who believe in arrested being, in retrogression, in eternal cycles, even those who believe in inanimate nature, and put her at the helm of the world, whatever be their native country, whatever be their language, they are not Germans, they are strangers to us, and one would hope that one day they would be wholly cut off from our people.

This, to do Fichte justice, was not a chauvinistic German sermon, because by Germans he meant, as Hegel meant, all the Germanic peoples; that makes it perhaps not very much better, but a little better. This category includes the French, it includes the English, it includes all the Nordic peoples, and it includes some of the Mediterranean peoples as well. Even so, the heart of the sermon is not simply patriotism, or simply an attempt to arouse the waning German spirit, crushed under the heel of Napoleon. The main thing is this broad distinction between those who are alive and those who are dead, those who are echoes and those who are voices, those who are annexes and those who are the genuine article, the genuine building. That is Fichte's fundamental distinction, and it bound its spell upon the mind of a great many young Germans born somewhere around the late 1770s and early 1780s.

The fundamental notion is not *cogito ergo sum* but *volo ergo sum*. Curiously enough, the French psychologist Maine de Biran, writing at about the same time, was developing the same kind of psychology – that personality was to be learned only through effort, through trying, through hurling yourself against some obstacle which made you feel yourself wholly. In other words you felt yourself properly only in a moment of resistance or opposition. Mastery, Titanism, is what this leads to as an ideal – both in private and in public life.

Let me say a few words – although it is very unjust to him to treat him so cursorily – about the somewhat analogous but in certain respects profoundly different doctrine of Fichte's younger contemporary Schelling, who had a greater influence on Coleridge, at any rate, than any other thinker, and a profound influence upon German thought as well, though he is very seldom read now, partly because most of his works appear today exceedingly opaque, not to say unintelligible.

Unlike Fichte, who contrasted the living principle of the human will with nature – which was, as to some extent in Kant, dead stuff, to be moulded, as opposed to some harmony to be fitted into – Schelling maintained a mystical vitalism. For him nature was itself something alive, a kind of spiritual self-development. He saw the world as beginning in a state of brute unconsciousness and gradually coming to consciousness of itself. Starting, as he says, from the most mysterious beginnings, from the dark, developing unconscious will, it gradually grows to self-consciousness. Nature is unconscious will; man is will come to consciousness of itself. Nature exhibits various stages of the will: every stage of nature is the will in some stage of its development. First there are the rocks and the earth, which are the will in a state of total unconsciousness. (This is an ancient Renaissance doctrine, to go no further, to gnostic sources.) Then gradually life enters into them, and there is the early life of the first biological species. Then come the plants, and after them the animals – the progressive self-consciousness, the progressive beating of the will through towards the realisation of some kind of purpose. Nature strives after something but is not aware that it strives for it. Man begins to strive and becomes aware of what he is striving for. By striving successfully for whatever it is that he may be striving for he brings the whole universe to higher consciousness of itself. For Schelling, God was a kind of self-developing principle of consciousness. Yes, he said, God is alpha and omega. Alpha is unconscious, omega is full consciousness come to itself. God is a kind of progressive phenomenon, a form of creative evolution – a notion which, indeed, Bergson made his own, for there is very little in Bergson's doctrine which was not previously in Schelling.

This is the doctrine which had a very profound influence upon German aesthetic philosophy and the philosophy of art; because if everything in nature is living, and if we ourselves are simply its most self-conscious representatives, the function of the artist is to delve within himself, and above all to delve within the dark and unconscious forces which move within him, and to bring these to consciousness by the most agonising and violent internal struggle. That is Schelling's doctrine. Nature does this too. There are struggles within nature. Every volcanic eruption, every phenomenon such as magnetism and electricity was interpreted by Schelling as being a struggle for self-assertion on the part of blind mysterious forces, except that in man they became half conscious. The only works of art, for him, which have any value at all – and this is a doctrine by which not only Coleridge but other art critics were subsequently influenced – are those which are similar to nature in conveying the pulsations of a not wholly conscious life. Any work of art which is fully self-conscious is for him a kind of photograph. Any work of art which is simply a copy, simply a piece of knowledge, something which, like science, is simply the product of careful observation and then of noting down in scrupulous terms what you have seen in a fully lucid, accurate and scientific manner – that is death. Life in a work of art is analogous with – is some kind of quality the work has in common with – what we admire in nature, namely some kind of power, force, energy, life, vitality bursting forth. That is why the great portraits, the great statues, the great works of music are called great, because we see in them not merely the surface, not merely the technique, not merely the form which the artist, perhaps consciously, imposed, but also something of which the artist may not be wholly aware, namely the pulsations within him of some kind of infinite spirit of which he happens to be the particularly articulate and self-conscious representative. The pulsations of this spirit are also, at a lower level, pulsations of nature, so that the work of art has the same vitalising effect upon the man who looks at it or who listens to it as certain phenomena of nature. When this is lacking, when the whole thing is wholly conventional, done according to rules, done in the full self-conscious blaze of complete awareness of what one is doing, the product is of necessity elegant, symmetrical and dead.

That is the fundamental romantic, anti-Enlightenment doctrine of art, and it has had a very considerable influence upon all critics who regard the unconscious as having some part to play, not merely as in the old Platonic theories of divine inspiration and the ecstatic artist who is not wholly aware of what he is doing – in Plato's doctrine in the *Ion* the god blows through the artist, who does not know what it is he is doing because something more powerful inspires him from outside – but upon all the doctrines which take an interest in, and regard it as valuable to consider, the unconscious or sub-conscious or pre-conscious element in the work either of the individual artist or of a group, a nation, a people, a culture. This goes directly back to Herder, who also regards folk-song and folk-dancing as the articulation of some kind of not wholly self-aware spirit within a nation, and worthless unless it is that.

It cannot be said that Schelling wrote these things down with a great deal of clarity. Nevertheless he wrote very rhapsodically and had a considerable effect upon his contemporaries. The first great doctrine which emerges from this combination of Fichte's doctrine of the will and Schelling's doctrine of the unconscious – the great formative factors in the aesthetic doctrine of the romantic movement, and subsequently its political and ethical doctrines as well – is the doctrine of symbolism. Symbolism is central in all romantic thought: that has always been noticed by all critics of the movement. Let me try to make it as clear as I am able, although I do not claim to understand it entirely, because, as Schelling very rightly says, romanticism is truly a wild wood, a labyrinth in which the only guiding thread is the will and the mood of a poet. As I am no poet I cannot altogether trust myself to provide a full exposition of this doctrine, though I shall do my best.

There are two kinds of symbols, to put it at its very simplest. There are conventional symbols and symbols of a somewhat different kind. Conventional symbols offer no difficulty. They are symbols which we invent for the purpose of meaning certain things, and there are rules about what they mean. Red and green traffic lights mean what they mean by convention. Red lights mean that motor cars may not pass, and they are simply another form of saying 'Do not pass.' 'Do not pass' is itself a form of symbolism, linguistic symbolism, which stands for some kind of ban on the part of persons in authority and holds within it some kind of threat, a perfectly understood threat that if you disobey this order dire consequences may follow. This is ordinary symbolism, examples of which are artificially invented languages, scientific treatises and any kind of conventional symbolism invented for a specific purpose, where the meaning of the symbol is laid down by rule.

But there are obviously symbols not quite of this kind. I do not wish to enter into the theory of symbolism in general, but, for my purposes, what these people meant by symbolism was the use of symbols for what could be expressed only symbolically and could not be expressed literally. The traffic situation is such that if instead of the green and red lights you were to put up signs saying 'Stop' or 'Go', or if instead of that you even placed persons of obvious authority to cry through megaphones 'Stop' and 'Go', this would serve its purpose equally well, at least so far as grammatical purposes are concerned. But if you ask, for example, in what sense a national flag waving in the wind, which arouses emotions in people's breasts, is a symbol, or in what sense the Marseillaise is a symbol, or, to go a little further, in what sense a Gothic cathedral built in a particular way, quite apart from its function as a building in which religious services occur, is a symbol for the particular religion which it houses, or in what sense sacred dances are symbols, or in what sense any kind of religious ritual is a symbol, or in what sense the Kaaba Stone is a great symbol to the Moslems, the answer will be that what these things symbolise is literally not expressible in any other way. Suppose someone asks, 'Would you spell out for me what it is that the word "England" stood for in the sentence "England expects every man to do his duty" when Nelson said it?' If you begin to spell it out, if you say 'England' means a certain number of featherless bipeds with reason, inhabiting a certain island at a particular moment in the early nineteenth century, clearly it does not mean that; it does not simply mean a group of persons, with names and addresses known to Nelson, whom he could if he wished, and took enough trouble, spell out. It plainly does not mean that, because the whole emotive force of the word 'England' extends over something both vaguer and more profound, and if you say 'What exactly is it that the word "England" stands for here? Would you unpack it, would you give me – however tedious it may be – the literal equivalent of what this is simply shorthand for?', this will not be easy to do. Nor will it be very easy to reply if you say 'What is it that the Kaaba Stone stands for? What is it that this particular prayer stands for? What is it that this cathedral means to the people who come to worship in it, apart from associations of a vaguely emotional kind, apart from a penumbra?' It is not simply that it arouses emotion: emotion might be aroused by the singing of birds; emotion might be aroused by a sunset; but a sunset is not a symbol and the singing of birds is not symbolic. To worshippers, however, a cathedral is a symbol, a religious rite is a symbol, the raising of the Host is a symbol.

The question now arises, what are these things symbolic of? The romantic doctrine was that there is an infinite striving forward on the part of reality, of the universe around us, that there is something which is infinite, something which is inexhaustible, of which the finite attempts to be the symbol but of course cannot. You seek to convey something which you can convey only by such means as you have at your command, but you know that this cannot convey the whole of what you are seeking to convey because this whole is literally infinite. That is why allegories and symbols are used. An allegory is a representation in words or in paint of something which has its own meaning but also stands for something other than itself. When an allegory stands for something other than itself, that which it stands for – for those who really believe in allegories and who say that the only mode of profound speech is allegorical, as Schelling believed, as the romantics in general believed – is *ex hypothesi* not statable itself. That is why the allegory has to be used, and that is why allegories and symbols are of necessity the only mode which I have of conveying that which I wish to convey.

What is it that I wish to convey? I wish to convey the stream of which Fichte speaks. I wish to convey something immaterial and I have to use material means for it. I have to convey something which is inexpressible and I have to use expression. I have to convey, perhaps, something unconscious and I have to use conscious means. I know in advance that I shall not succeed and cannot succeed, and therefore all I can do is to get nearer and nearer in some asymptotic approach; I do my best, but it is an agonising struggle in which, if I am an artist, or indeed for the German romantics any kind of self-conscious thinker, I am engaged for the whole of my life.

This is something to do with the notion of depth. The notion of depth is something with which philosophers seldom deal. Nevertheless it is a concept perfectly susceptible to treatment and indeed one of the most important of the categories that we use. When we say that a work is profound or deep, quite apart from the fact that this is obviously a metaphor, I suppose from wells, which are profound and deep – when one says that someone is a profound writer, or that a picture or a work of music is profound, it is not very clear what we mean, but we certainly do not wish to exchange these descriptions for some other term such as 'beautiful' or 'important' or 'constructed according to rules' or even 'immortal'. When I say that Pascal is more profound than Descartes (although Descartes, no doubt, was a man of genius), or that Dostoevsky, whom I may or may not like, is a more profound writer than Tolstoy, whom I may like much better, or that Kafka is a more profound writer than Hemingway, what exactly am I trying unsuccessfully to convey by means of this metaphor, which remains metaphorical because I have nothing better that I can use? According to the romantics – and this is one of their principal contributions to understanding in general – what I mean by depth, although they do not discuss it under that name, is inexhaustibility, unembraceability. In the case of works of art that are beautiful but not profound, or even of pieces of prose fiction or philosophy, I can translate into perfectly lucid literal terms; I can explain to you, say, about some musical work of the eighteenth century, well constructed, melodious, agreeable, even perhaps a work of genius, why it is made in the way it is, and even why it gives pleasure. I can tell you that human beings feel a particular kind of pleasure in listening to certain kinds of harmonies. I can describe this pleasure, perhaps quite minutely, by all kinds of ingenious introspective devices. If I am a marvellous describer – if I am Proust, if I am Tolstoy, if I am a well-trained descriptive psychologist – I might succeed in giving you some kind of version of your actual emotions when listening to a particular piece of music or reading a particular piece of prose, a version which is sufficiently similar to what you are in fact feeling or thinking at this particular moment to be regarded as an adequate prose translation of what is occurring: scientific, true, objective, verifiable and so on. But in the case of works which are profound the more I say the more remains to be said. There is no doubt that, although I attempt to describe what their profundity consists in, as soon as I speak it becomes quite clear that, no matter how long I speak, new chasms open. No matter what I say I always have to leave three dots at the end. Whatever description I give always opens the doors to something further, something even darker, perhaps, but certainly something which is in principle incapable of being reduced to precise, clear, verifiable, objective prose. That being so, this is certainly one of the uses of 'profound' – to invoke the notion of irreducibility, the notion that I am forced in my discussion, forced in description, to use language which is in principle, not only today but for ever, inadequate for its purpose.

Suppose I am trying to explain a particular profound proposition. I do my best, but I know that it cannot be exhausted; and the more inexhaustible it seems to me to be – the wider the region to which it seems to me to apply, the more chasms open, the deeper the chasms are, the wider the area on which they open – the more liable I am to say that this particular proposition is profound and not merely true or interesting or amusing or original, or whatever

103

else I might be tempted to say. When, for example, Pascal makes the famous remark that the heart has its reasons as well as the head, when Goethe says that no matter how hard we try there will always be an irreducible element of anthropomorphism in everything we do and think, these remarks strike people as profound for this reason, because wherever we apply them they open new vistas, and these vistas are not reducible, not embraceable, not describable, not collectable; you have no formula which will by deduction lead you to all of them. This is the fundamental notion of depth in the romantics, and it is to this, in a large degree, that most of their talk about the finite standing for the infinite, the material standing for the immaterial, the dead standing for the living, space standing for time, words standing for something which is in itself wordless, relates. 'Can the sacred be seized?' asked Friedrich Schlegel, and he replied, 'No, it can never be seized because the mere imposition of form deforms it.' This is what runs through their entire theory of life and of art.

This leads to two quite interesting and obsessive phenomena which are then very present both in nineteenth- and in twentieth-century thought and feeling. One is nostalgia, and the other is paranoia of a certain kind. The nostalgia is due to the fact that, since the infinite cannot be exhausted, and since we are seeking to embrace it, nothing that we do will ever satisfy us. When Novalis was asked where he thought he was tending, what his art was about, he said 'I am always going home, always to my father's house.' This was in one sense a religious remark, but he also meant that all these attempts at the exotic, the strange, the foreign, the odd, all these attempts to emerge from the empirical framework of daily life, the writing of fantastic stories with transformations and transmogrifications of a most peculiar kind, attempts at writing down stories which are symbolic or allegorical or contain all kinds of mystical and veiled references, esoteric imagery of a most peculiar kind which has preoccupied critics for years, are all attempts to go back, to go home to what is pulling and drawing him, the famous infinite *Sehnsucht* of the romantics, the search for the blue flower, as Novalis called it. The search for the blue flower is an attempt either to absorb the infinite into myself, to make myself at one with it, or to dissolve myself into it. This is a secularised version, obviously, of that profound religious striving towards being at one with God, of reviving the Christ within me, of making myself one with some of the creative forces of nature in some pagan sense, which comes to the Germans from Plato, from Eckhart, from Boehme, from German mysticism, from a number of other sources, except that here it takes a literary and a secular form.

This nostalgia is the very opposite of what the Enlightenment regarded as its special contribution. The Enlightenment supposed that there was a closed, perfect pattern of life, as I have tried to explain. There was some particular form of life and of art, and of feeling and of thought, which was correct, which was right, which was true and objective and could be taught to people if only we knew enough. There was some kind of solution to our problems, and if only we could construct a structure which accorded with the solution and then proceed to fit ourselves, to put it crudely, into the structure, we should obtain answers both to problems of thought and to problems of action. But if this is not so, if *ex hypothesi* the universe is in movement and not at rest, if it is a form of activity and not a lump of stuff, if it is infinite and not finite, if it is constantly varying and never still, never the same (to use these various metaphors which the romantics constantly use), if it is a constant wave (as Friedrich Schlegel says), how can we possibly even try to describe it? What are we to do when we wish to describe a wave? We usually end up by producing a stagnant pool. When we try to describe the light we can describe it accurately only by putting it out. Therefore do not let us attempt to describe it. But you cannot not attempt to describe it, because that means to stop expressing, and to stop expressing is to stop living. For these romantics, to live is to do something, to do is to express your nature. To express your nature is to express your relation to the universe. Your relation to the universe is inexpressible, but you must nevertheless express it. This is the agony, this is the problem. This is the unending *Sehnsucht*, this is the yearning, this is the reason why we must go to distant countries, this is why we seek for exotic examples, this is why we travel in the East and write novels about the past, this is why we indulge in all manner of fantasies. That is the typical romantic nostalgia. If the home for which they are seeking, if the harmony, the perfection about which they talk could be granted to them, they would reject it. It is in principle, by definition, something to which an approach can be made but which cannot be seized, because that is the nature of reality. One is reminded of the famous cynical story about someone who said to Dante Gabriel Rossetti when he was writing about the Holy Grail, 'But Mr Rossetti, when you have found the Grail, what will you do with it?' This is precisely the typical question which the romantics knew very well how to answer. In their case the Grail was in principle both undiscoverable and such that one's whole life could not be prevented from being a perpetual search for it, and that is because of the nature of the universe, such as it is. It might have been different, but it is not. The brute fact about the universe is that it is not fully expressible, it is not fully exhaustible, it is not at rest, it is in motion; this is the basic datum, and this is what we discover when we discover that the self is something of which we are aware only in effort. Effort is action, action is movement, movement is unfinishable – perpetual movement. That is the fundamental romantic image, which I am trying to convey, as best I can, in words, which *ex hypothesi* cannot convey it.

The second notion, that of paranoia, is somewhat different. There is an optimistic version of romanticism in which what the romantics feel is that by going forward, by expanding our nature, by destroying the obstacles in our path, whatever they may be – the dead French rules of the eighteenth century, political and economic institutions of a destructive kind, laws, authority, any kind of cut and dried truth, any kind of rules or institutions which are regarded as absolute, perfect, unappealable from – we are liberating ourselves more and more and allowing our infinite nature to soar to greater and greater heights and become wider, deeper, freer, more vital, more like the divinity towards which it strives. But there is another, more pessimistic version of this, which obsesses the twentieth century to some extent. There is a notion that although we individuals seek to liberate ourselves, yet the universe is not to be tamed in this easy fashion. There is something behind, there is something in the dark depths of the unconscious, or of history; there is something, at any rate, not seized by us which frustrates our dearest wishes. Sometimes it is conceived as a kind of indifferent or even hostile nature, sometimes as the cunning of history, which optimists think bears us towards ever more glorious goals, but which pessimists such as Schopenhauer think is simply a huge fathomless ocean of undirected will upon which we bob like a little boat with no direction, no possibility of really understanding the element in which we are, or directing our course upon it; and this is a huge, powerful, ultimately hostile force, to resist which or even to come to terms with which is never of the slightest use.

This paranoia takes all kinds of other, sometimes much cruder, forms. It takes the form, for example, of looking for all kinds of conspiracies in history. People begin to think that perhaps history is formed by forces over which we have no control. Someone is at the back of it all: perhaps the Jesuits, perhaps the Jews, perhaps the Freemasons. This attitude was much stimulated by attempts to explain the course of the French Revolution. We the enlightened, we the virtuous, we the wise, we the good and the kind seek to do this or that, but somehow all our efforts end in nothing, and therefore there must be some fearful hostile force lying in wait for us which trips us up when we are on the brink, as we think, of great success. This view takes, as I say, crude forms, such as the conspiracy theory of history, by which you always look for concealed enemies, sometimes for larger and larger conceptions such as economic forces, the forces of production or class war (as in Marx), or the much vaguer and more metaphysical notion of the cunning of reason or of history (as in Hegel), which understands its goal much better than we do and plays tricks upon us. Hegel says, 'The spirit cheats us, the spirit intrigues, the spirit lies, the spirit triumphs.' He almost conceives of it as a kind of huge, ironical, Aristophanic force which mocks the poor human beings who are trying to construct their little homes upon the slopes of what they regard as a green and flowery mountain, but which turns out to be the vast volcano of human history, which is about to erupt once again, ultimately perhaps for human good, ultimately in order to realise itself towards an ideal, but in the short run destroying a large number of innocent persons and causing a great deal of suffering and damage.

This too is a romantic idea, because once you get the notion that there is outside us something larger, something unseizable, something unobtainable, you either have feelings towards it of love, as Fichte wanted, or of fear; and if you have feelings of fear, the fear becomes paranoiac. This paranoia goes on accumulating in the nineteenth century: it accumulates to a height in Schopenhauer, it dominates the works of Wagner, and it comes to an immense climax in all kinds of works in the twentieth century obsessed by the thought that, no matter what we do, there is some canker, there is a worm in the bud somewhere, there is something which dooms us to perpetual frustration, whether it be human beings whom we must exterminate or impersonal forces against which all effort is useless. Works by writers such as Kafka are filled with a peculiar sense of undirected *angst*, of terror, of basic apprehension, which is not fixated upon any identifiable object; and this is very true about the early romantic works as well. Tieck's stories, *Der blonde Eckbert* for example, are pervaded by terror. No doubt they are meant to be allegories, but what always happens is that the hero begins by living happily and then something terrible happens. A golden bird appears before him and sings a song about *Waldein-samkeit*, which is already a romantic concept – about solitude in the woods of a half delightful and half terrifying sort. Then he kills the bird and various misfortunes follow, and he goes on killing, he goes on destroying, he gets enmeshed in a frightful net which some awful mysterious force has laid for him. He seeks to liberate himself from it. He murders more, he struggles, he fights, he goes under. This kind of nightmare is extremely typical of early German romantic writing and it comes from exactly the same source, namely the notion of the will as dominating life – the will, not reason, not an order of things which can be studied and therefore controlled, but some kind of will. So long as it is my will, and a will directed towards ends which I myself manufacture, it is presumably benevolent. So long as it is the will of a benevolent deity or the will of a history which is guaranteed to bring me to a happy conclusion, as it is in the writings of all the optimistic historical philosophers, that presumably is not too terrifying. But it may turn out that the end is much blacker and more terrifying and more unfathomable than I think. In this way the romantics tend to oscillate between extremes of mystical optimism and appalling pessimism, which gives their writings a peculiar kind of uneven quality.

The second of the three great influences identified by Schlegel was the French Revolution. This had an obvious effect upon the Germans, because it led, as a result of the Napoleonic wars in particular, to a vast burst of wounded national feeling, which fed the stream of romanticism, in so far as it was an assertion of the national will, come what may. But what I wish to stress is not this aspect of it; but rather that the French Revolution, although it promised a perfect solution to human ills, being founded, as I have said, upon peaceful universalism – the doctrine of unimpeded progress, whose goal was to be classical perfection, which, once we arrived at it, would last for ever upon some kind of adamantine foundations laid by human reason – nevertheless did not go the way it was intended (that was clear to all), and therefore what it attracted attention to was not at all reason, peace, harmony, universal freedom, equality, liberty, fraternity – not the things which it was set in train to satisfy – but, on the contrary, violence, appalling, unpredictable change in human affairs, the irrationality of mobs, the enormous power of individual heroes, great men, evil and good, who were able to dominate these mobs and alter the course of history in all kinds of ways. It is the poetry of action and battle and death which the French Revolution stimulated in people's minds and imaginations, not merely in Germany but everywhere, and therefore it had an effect exactly opposite to that which it was intended to have. In particular it stimulated the notion of a mysterious nine-tenths of the iceberg, about which we did not know enough.

It was naturally bound to be asked why the French Revolution was a failure, in the sense that after it, fairly conspicuously, the majority of Frenchmen were not free, not equal and not particularly fraternal – at any rate a number sufficiently large to cause the question to be asked. Although, no doubt, the lot of some of them had been improved, the lot of others had obviously deteriorated. In neighbouring countries too, although some persons had been liberated, other persons did not feel that this had been worthwhile.

Various answers were given. Those who believed in economics

said that the political makers of the Revolution ignored economic facts. Those who believed in the monarchy or the Church said that the deepest instincts and the deepest faith of human nature had been flouted by atheistical materialism, which had naturally produced consequences of a dreadful kind, and this was, perhaps, simply the punishment of human nature or of God (depending on your particular philosophy) upon some kind of defiance of it. But what the Revolution led everybody to suspect was that perhaps not enough was known: the doctrines of the French *philosophes*, which were supposedly a blueprint for the alteration of society in any desired direction, had in fact proved inadequate. Therefore, although the upper portion of human social life was visible – to economists, psychologists, moralists, writers, students, every kind of scholar and observer of the facts – that portion was merely the tip of some huge iceberg of which a vast section was sunk beneath the ocean. This invisible section had been taken for granted a little too blandly, and had therefore avenged itself by producing all kinds of exceedingly unexpected consequences.

The notion of unintended consequences, the notion that although you propose, the hidden reality disposes, although you alter it, nevertheless it suddenly straightens itself and strikes you in the face; that if you try to alter these things too much – nature, men, whatever it is – then something called 'human nature' or 'the nature of society' or 'the dark forces of the unconscious' or 'the forces of production' or 'the Idea' – it does not matter what the name of this vast entity is – proceeds to strike you, and strike you down – that ate itself into the imagination of a great many persons in Europe who would certainly not have described themselves as romantics, and fed the streams of all kinds of theodicies: the Marxist theodicy, the Hegelian theodicy, Spengler's theodicy, Toynbee's theodicy, and a great many other theological writings of our time. This, I think, is where this notion begins; and it fed the stream of paranoia also, in that it again conjured up the notion of something stronger than us, some huge impersonal force, which could be neither investigated nor deflected. This did make the whole universe far more terrifying than it had been in the eighteenth century.

The third of Schlegel's influences was Goethe's novel *Wilhelm*

Meister. The romantics admired this not so much for its power of storytelling, but for two other reasons: first of all, because it was an account of the self-formation of a man of genius – of how a man can take himself in hand and by the free exercise of his noble and unrestrained will make himself into something. This is presumably the creative autobiography of Goethe as an artist. But more than that, they also liked the fact that there were very sharp transitions in the novel. From a piece of sober prose, or a scientific description of, say, the temperature of water or a particular kind of garden, Goethe suddenly goes off into ecstatic, poetical, lyrical accounts of one kind and another and bursts into poetry and then as sharply and as quickly returns to perfectly melodious but severe prose. These sharp transitions from poetry to prose, from ecstasy to scientific descriptions, appear to the romantics to be a marvellous weapon for the purpose of blowing up an over-set reality. This is how works of art should be written. They should not be written in accordance with rules, they should not be copies of some kind of given nature, of some *rerum natura*, some kind of structure of things of which the work of art is an explanation, or, worse still, a copy or a photograph. The business of a work of art is to liberate us, and it liberates us by ignoring the superficial symmetries of nature, the superficial rules, and by sharp transitions from one mode into another – from poetry to prose, from theology to botany or whatever – knocks down a great many of the conventional divisions by which we are hemmed in and cribbed and imprisoned.

I do not think that Goethe regarded this as at all a valid analysis of his work. He looked with a certain nervousness upon these romantics, whom he, and Schiller too, regarded as rather rootless Bohemians, third-rate artists (which some of them certainly were), persons of rather wild and inconsequential life whom nevertheless, because they admired him so much and worshipped him so well, he did not wish altogether to despise or to ignore. And so a somewhat ambivalent relationship grew up between them, such that they admired him as the greatest of German geniuses, but despised his philistine tastes, despised his kotowing to the Grand Duke of Weimar, regarded him as having sold out in many ways – as having started as a bold and original genius but ended as a kind of silken courtier. On the other hand he looked upon them as poor artists, covering up a lack of creative genius by an unnecessary wildness of expression, but at the same time Germans, admirers, the only audience which, for a time, he had, and therefore not to be neglected, not to be kicked away too recklessly. That, roughly, was the relation between them. It remained a very uncomfortable relation until the end of Goethe's life, and certainly Goethe himself never lent himself to romanticism. Towards the end of his life he said 'Romanticism is disease, classicism is health', and that is his fundamental sermon.

Even *Faust* (which the romantics did not particularly admire), although the hero goes through all kinds of romantic transformations, and is tossed upon the wild wave – there are a great many passages in which it is clear that he is compared to a wild and rushing torrent, leaping from rock to rock, constantly thirsting for new experiences provided by Mephistopheles – is in the end a drama of reconciliation. The point about Faust, after he has killed Gretchen, after he has killed Philemon and Baucis, after he has performed a good many crimes both in Part 1 and in Part 2, is that there is some kind of harmonious release and resolution of all these conflicts, although no doubt they have cost a great deal of blood and suffering. But blood and suffering were nothing to Goethe: like Hegel he supposed that the divine harmonies could be made only by sharp clashes, by violent disharmonies, which from a greater height would have been perceived as contributory factors to some enormous harmony. But that is not romantic; if anything it is anti-romantic, because the general tendency of Goethe is to say that there is a solution – a hard, difficult solution, perhaps to be perceived only by the mystical eye, but nevertheless a solution. Goethe also, in his novels, preached exactly what the romantics detested. In *Hermann und Dorothea* and in *Die Wahlverwandtschaften* the whole sermon is that if an emotional knot occurs, if there is some kind of fearful complication between, let us say, a married woman and her lover, on no account may the easy solution of divorce, or the abandonment of wedlock, be adopted, but on the contrary resignation, suffering, bowing to the yoke of convention, preservation of the pillars of society. The sermon is essentially that of order, self-restraint, discipline and the crushing of any kind of chaotic or anti-legal factors.

This to the romantics was absolute poison. There is nothing they dislike more. In their own private lives they were, some of them, somewhat disorderly. The *cénacle*, the little group of romantics who gathered in Jena – the two brothers Schlegel, for a time Fichte, for a time Schleiermacher in Berlin, and Schelling – believed and preached in the most violent terms the duties and the importance of total freedom, including free love. August Wilhelm Schlegel married a lady because she was about to have a child – she was a revolutionary German lady of considerable intellect, imprisoned for a time by the Germans in Mainz for having collaborated with the French revolutionaries – and then with graceful feelings yielded her up to Schelling. This occurred earlier, too, in the case of Schiller and Jean Paul, though no marriage actually took place. Examples could be multiplied. But quite apart from their personal relationships, the great novel which incorporated their view of life, and which shocked Goethe and Hegel profoundly, though it is not perhaps a work of great literary merit, was *Lucinde*, published by Friedrich Schlegel at the end of the eighteenth century, and a kind of *Lady Chatterley* of its time. It was a highly erotic novel, giving very violent descriptions indeed of various types of lovemaking, as well as containing sermons of a romantic kind about the necessity of freedom and self-expression.

The heart of *Lucinde*, quite apart from its erotic side, is the description of what a free relationship between human beings can be. In particular, analogies are constantly made with a little baby called Wilhelmine, who throws her legs in the air in a very free and unrestrained manner. The hero exclaims and says: 'This is how one should live! Here is a little child, naked and unrestrained by convention. It wears no clothes, it bows to no authority, it believes in no conventional directors of its life, and above all it is idle, it has no task to do. Idleness is the last spark that is left to us from the divine paradise from which humanity was once expelled. Freedom, the capacity to throw one's legs in the air, to do anything one wishes, that is the last privilege that we have in this fearful world, this awful causal treadmill when nature presses upon us with such fearful savagery' – and so on.

The novel caused very profound shock and was defended by the great Berlin preacher, Schleiermacher, in terms not altogether unreminiscent of the defence by various British clergymen of *Lady Chatterley's Lover* in the 1960s. That is to say, just as Lawrence's book was represented, so far from being anti-spiritual in character, as moving in the same direction as, almost as a prop of, Christian orthodoxy, so *Lucinde*, which was a pornographic novel of the fourth order, was represented by the loyal Schleiermacher as being entirely spiritual in character. All its physical descriptions were described as allegorical, and everything in it was simply said to be a great sermon, a hymn to the spiritual freedom of man, no longer shackled by false convention. Later in life Schleiermacher tended to retreat from this position, which probably does greater credit to his kindness and his loyalty and his generosity of heart than to his critical acumen. Be that as it may, the purpose of *Lucinde* was to break down conventions. Wherever you could break down conventions you must do so.

Perhaps the most interesting and acute case of the breaking down of conventions is to be found in the plays of Tieck and the stories of the famous storyteller E. T. A. Hoffmann. The general proposition of the eighteenth century, indeed of all previous centuries, as I tirelessly repeat, is that there is a nature of things, there is a *rerum natura*, there is a structure of things. For the romantics this was profoundly false. There was no structure of things because that would hem us in, that would suffocate us. There must be a field for action. The potential is more real than the actual. What is made is dead. Once you have constructed a work of art, abandon it, because once it is constructed it is there, it is done for, it is last year's calendar. What is made, what has been constructed, what has been already understood must be abandoned. Glimpses, fragments, intimations, mystical illumination – that is the only way to seize reality, because any attempt to circumscribe it, any attempt to give a coherent account, any attempt to be harmonious, to have a beginning and a middle and an end, is essentially a perversion and a caricature of what is in its essence chaotic and shapeless, a beating stream, a tremendous great stream of self-realising will, the idea of imprisoning which is absurd and blasphemous. That is the real fervid centre of romantic faith.

There is a story by Hoffmann about a perfectly decent city councillor, a book collector, who sits in a dressing-gown in his room, surrounded in a normal way by old manuscripts, and outside his door there is a brass knocker. The brass knocker, however, at times turns into a hideous apple-vendor: sometimes she is an apple-vendor and sometimes a brass knocker. The brass knocker sometimes winks like the apple-vendor, the apple-vendor occasionally behaves like a brass knocker. As for her master, the respectable councillor, sometimes he sits in his chair, sometimes he gets into a bowl of punch and disappears into its steam and goes up in the air with the spirits; or occasionally he dissolves himself in the punch and gets drunk by other people and has peculiar adventures thereafter. This for Hoffmann is an ordinary sort of fantastic story, for which he was very famous; whenever you begin a story by him you can never tell what may happen. There is a cat in the room. The cat may be a cat, but it may of course also be a transformed human being. The cat cannot quite tell; he tells you that he cannot quite tell; and this casts a certain air of uncertainty over all the proceedings, which is perfectly deliberate. When Hoffmann was walking across a bridge in Berlin he often felt as if he was encapsulated in a glass bottle. He was not sure whether the people he saw round him were human beings or dolls. This I think was a genuine piece of psychological delusion – he was in some respects psychologically not wholly normal – but at the same time the primary motif in his fiction is always the transformability of everything into everything.

Tieck writes a play, *Puss in Boots*, in which the King says to the Prince who comes to see him, 'You who come from so far away, how is it you speak our language so well?', to which the Prince says 'Hush!' The King says, 'Why do you say "Hush!"?', and the Prince says, 'If I do not – if you do not cease talking about the subject – the play cannot continue.' Then some member of the audience is made to get up and say, 'But this is the flouting of all possible rules of realism, it is intolerable that characters should discuss the play between them.' This is very deliberate. In another play by Tieck a man, Scaramouche, is riding on a donkey.

Suddenly there is a thunderstorm, and he says 'But there's nothing about this in the play; there's nothing about rain in my part, I'm getting very wet.' He rings the bell and the mechanic comes in. He says to the mechanic, 'Why is it raining?' The mechanic says, 'The audience likes thunderstorms', to which Scaramouche says, 'In dignified historical plays it cannot rain.' The mechanic says, 'Yes it can', produces examples, and says that anyhow he has been paid to make it rain. Then someone gets up in the audience and says, 'You must cease this intolerable bickering, the play must have some degree of illusion. It is quite impossible for a play to go on and for characters in it to discuss its technique' – and so on. In the very same play there is a play within a play, and within that play another play; the audiences of all three plays talk to each other, and in particular one person who stands somewhat outside the play discusses the relations of the various audiences to each other.

This of course has its analogues: it is the predecessor of Pirandello, of Dadaism, of surrealism, of the theatre of the absurd – this is where it all begins. The point of it is to try to confuse reality with appearance as far as possible, to break down the barrier between illusion and reality, between dreams and waking, between night and day, between the conscious and the unconscious, in order to produce a sense of the absolutely unbarred universe, of the wall-less universe, and of perpetual change, perpetual transformation, out of which someone with a powerful will can mould, if only temporarily, anything he pleases. That is the central doctrine of the romantic movement, and naturally it has its political analogue as well. Romantic political authors begin to say, 'The State is not a machine, the State is not a gadget. If the State were a machine people would have thought of something else, but they have not. The State is either a natural growth or it is an emanation of some mysterious primal force which we cannot understand and which has some kind of theological authority.' Adam Müller says that Christ died not only for individuals but for States, which was a very extreme statement of theological politics, and then explains that the State is a mystical institution profoundly rooted in the deepest possible, the least fathomable and the least intelligible aspects of human existence, which was essentially in perpetual criss-crossing movement; the attempt to reduce this to constitutions, to laws, is doomed to failure because nothing written lives; no constitution, if it is written, can possibly survive, because writing is dead and the constitution must be a living flame within the hearts of human beings who live together as one passionate mystical family. When that kind of talk begins this doctrine starts to penetrate into regions for which it was perhaps not originally intended, and there, naturally, it begins to have very serious consequences.

I turn finally, very briefly, to the concept of romantic irony, which is exactly the same. Irony was invented by Friedrich Schlegel: the idea is that whenever you see honest citizens setting about their business, whenever you see a well-composed poem – a poem composed according to the rules – whenever you see a peaceful institution which protects the lives and property of citizens, laugh at it, mock at it, be ironical, blow it up, point out that the opposite is equally true. The only weapon there is against death, for him, against ossification and against any form of the stabilisation and freezing of the life stream is what he calls *Ironie*. It is an obscure concept but the general notion is that, corresponding to any proposition that anyone may utter, there must be at least three other propositions, each of which is contrary to it, and each of which is equally true, all of which must be believed, particularly because they are contradictory – because that is the only way of escaping from the hideous logical strait-jacket which he is frightened of, whether in the form of physical causality, or of State-created laws, or of aesthetic rules about how to compose poems, or of rules of perspective or rules of historical painting or rules of other kinds of painting laid down by various mandarins in France in the eighteenth century. This must be escaped from. It cannot be escaped by simply denying the rules, because a denial will simply bring about another orthodoxy, another set of rules contradictory of the original rules. Rules must be blown up as such.

These two elements – the free untrammelled will and the denial of the fact that there is a nature of things, the attempt to blow up and explode the very notion of a stable structure of anything – are the deepest and in a sense the most insane elements in this extremely valuable and important movement.

6

THE LASTING EFFECTS

I NOW PROPOSE to say, however rash it may seem, what the heart of romanticism appears to me to be. I should like to go back again to a theme which I introduced earlier, namely the old tradition which is at the heart of all Western thought for at least two thousand years and more, before the middle of the eighteenth century – that particular attitude, those particular beliefs, which, it appears to me, romanticism attacked and gravely damaged. I mean the old proposition that virtue is knowledge, a proposition which was explicitly enunciated, I suppose, for the first time by Socrates in the pages of Plato, and which is common to him and to the Christian tradition. What kind of knowledge, one may disagree about: there are battles between one philosopher and another, one religion and another, one scientist and another, between religion and science, between religion and art, between every kind of attitude and every kind of school of thought and every other, but the battle is invariably about what that true knowledge of reality is, the possession of which makes it possible for men to know what to do, how to fit in. It is agreed that there is a nature of things such that, if you know this nature, and know yourself in relation to this nature, and, if there is a divinity, you know this divinity, and understand the relationships between everything that composes the universe, then your goals as well as the facts about yourself must become clear to you, and you understand what it is that you should do if you are to fulfil yourself in the manner in which your nature cries out for you to do so. For this it is necessary to know whether this knowledge is knowledge of physics or psychology or theology, or some intuitive kind of knowledge, individual or public, whether it is confined to experts or may be known by every man. About all these things disagreement may occur, but that there is such knowledge – that is the foundation of the entire Western tradition, which, as I say, romanticism attacked. The view is that of a jigsaw puzzle of which we must fit in the fragments, of a secret treasure which we must seek.

The essence of this view is that there is a body of facts to which we must submit. Science is submission, science is being guided by the nature of things, scrupulous regard for what there is, non-deviation from the facts, understanding, knowledge, adaptation. The opposite of this, which is what the romantic movement proclaimed, may be summarised under two heads. One of these will by now be familiar, namely the notion of the indomitable will: not knowledge of values, but their creation, is what men achieve. You create values, you create goals, you create ends, and in the end you create your own vision of the universe, exactly as artists create works of art – and before the artist has created a work of art, it does not exist, it is not anywhere. There is no copying, there is no adaptation, there is no learning of the rules, there is no external check, there is no structure which you must understand and adapt yourself to before you can proceed. The heart of the entire process is invention, creation, making, out of literally nothing, or out of any materials that may be to hand. The most central aspect of this view is that your universe is as you choose to make it, to some degree at any rate; that is the philosophy of Fichte, that is to some extent the philosophy of Schelling, that is the insight, indeed, in our own century even of such psychologists as Freud, who maintain that the universe of people possessed by one set of illusions or fantasies will be different from the universe of those possessed by another.

The second proposition – connected with the first – is that there is no structure of things. There is no pattern to which you must adapt yourself. There is only, if not the flow, the endless self-creativity of the universe. The universe must not be conceived of as a set of facts, as a pattern of events, as a collection of lumps in space, three-dimensional entities bound together by certain unbreakable relations, as taught to us by physics, chemistry and other natural sciences; the universe is a process of perpetual

forward self-thrusting, perpetual self-creation, which can be conceived of either as hostile to man, as by Schopenhauer or even to
some extent by Nietzsche, so that it will overthrow all human
efforts to check it, to organise it, to feel at home in it, to make
oneself some kind of cosy pattern in which one can rest – either in
that way, or as friendly, because by identifying yourself with it, by
creating with it, by throwing yourself into this great process,
indeed by discovering in yourself those very creative forces which
you also discover outside, by identifying on the one hand spirit, on
the other hand matter, by seeing the whole thing as a vast self-
organising and self-creative process, you will at last be free.

'Understanding' is not the proper term to use, because it always
presupposes the understander and the understood, the knower and
the known, some kind of gap between the subject and the object;
but here there is no object, there is only the subject, thrusting itself
forward. The subject may be the universe, or the individual, or the
class, the nation, the Church – whatever is identified as the truest
reality of which the universe consists. But in any case it is a process
of perpetual forward creation, and all schemas, all generalisations,
all patterns imposed upon it are forms of distortion, forms of
breaking. When Wordsworth said that to dissect is to murder, this
is approximately what he meant; and he was much the mildest of
those who expressed this point of view.

To ignore this, to evade it, to attempt to see things as submissive
to some kind of intellectualisation, some sort of plan, to attempt to
draw up a set of rules, or a set of laws, or a formula, is a form of
self-indulgence, and in the end suicidal stupidity. That at any rate is
the sermon of the romantics. Whenever you try to understand
anything, by whatever powers you have, you will discover, as I
have tried to explain, that what you are pursuing is inexhaustible,
that you are trying to catch the uncatchable, that you are trying to
apply a formula to something which evades your formula, because
wherever you try to nail it down, new abysses open, and these
abysses open to yet other abysses. The only persons who have ever
made sense of reality are those who understand that to try to
circumscribe things, to try to nail them down, to try to describe
them, no matter how scrupulously, is a vain task. This will be true
not only of science, which does this by means of the most rigorous

generalisations of (to the romantics) the most external and empty kind, but even of scrupulous writers, scrupulous describers of experience – realists, naturalists, those who belong to the school of the flow of consciousness: Proust, Tolstoy, the most gifted diviners of every movement of the human spirit – even of those, to the extent to which they commit themselves to some kind of objective description, whether by external inspection, or by the most subtle introspection, the most subtle insight into the inner movements of the spirit. So long as they labour under the illusion that it is possible once and for all to write down, to describe, to give any finality to the process which they are trying to catch, which they are trying to nail down, unreality and fantasy will result – an attempt, always, to cage the uncageable, to pursue truth where there is no truth, to stop the unceasing flow, to catch movement by means of rest, to catch time by means of space, to catch light by means of darkness. That is the romantic sermon.

When they asked themselves how, in that case, one could begin to understand reality, in some sense of the word 'understand', how one might obtain some kind of insight into it without positively distinguishing oneself on the one hand as a subject, and reality on the other hand as an object, without in the process killing it, the answer which they sought to give, at least some of them, was that the only way of doing this was by means of myths, by means of those symbols which I have touched on, because myths embody within themselves something inarticulable, and also manage to encapsulate the dark, the irrational, the inexpressible, that which conveys the deep darkness of this whole process, in images which themselves carry you to further images and which themselves point in some infinite direction. That at any rate is what the Germans, who are in the end responsible for this whole outlook, preached. For them the Greeks understood life because Apollo and Dionysus were symbols, they were myths, who conveyed certain properties, and yet if you asked yourself what it was that Apollo stood for, what it was that Dionysus wanted, the attempt to spell this out in a finite number of words, or even to paint a finite number of pictures, was plainly an absurdity. Therefore myths are at one and the same time images which the mind can contemplate, in relative tranquillity, and yet also something which is everlasting, follows each generation, transforms itself with the transformation of men, and is an inexhaustible supply of the relevant images, which are at once static and eternal.

But these Greek images are dead for us, for we are not Greeks. That much Herder had taught them. The notion of returning to Dionysus or Odin is absurd. Therefore we must have modern myths, and since there are no modern myths, because science has killed them, or at any rate has made the atmosphere unpropitious to them, we must create them. As a result there is a conscious process of myth-making: we find, in the early nineteenth century, a conscientious and painful effort to construct myths – or perhaps not so painful, perhaps some of it could be described as spontaneous – which will serve us in the way in which the old myths served the Greeks. 'The roots of life are lost in darkness,' said August Wilhelm Schlegel; 'the magic of life rests on insoluble mystery', and this is what the myths must incorporate. 'The romantic art', said his brother Friedrich, 'is ... a perpetual becoming without ever attaining to perfection. Nothing can plumb its depths ... It alone is infinite, alone free; its first law is the will of the creator, the will of the creator that knows no law.' All art is an attempt to evoke by symbols the inexpressible vision of the unceasing activity which is life. This is what I have attempted to convey.

That is how *Hamlet*, for example, becomes a myth, or *Don Quixote*, or *Faust*. What Shakespeare would have said about the extraordinary literature which has accumulated around *Hamlet*, what Cervantes would have said about the extraordinary adventures which Don Quixote has had from the early nineteenth century onwards, I do not know, but at any rate these works were converted into rich sources of mythology, and if their inventors knew nothing about it, so much the better. The assumption was that the author cannot know what dark depths he plumbs. Mozart cannot tell what genius it is that inspires him; indeed, so far as he can tell, his genius probably to that extent dries up. If you wish for a very vivid illustration of the myth-making capacity of the early nineteenth century, which is the heart of the romantic movement – the attempt to break reality into fragments, to get away from the structure of things, to say the unsayable – the history of Mozart's opera *Don Giovanni* is quite apt.

As everyone who has heard it knows, the opera ends, or almost ends, with the destruction of Don Giovanni by the infernal forces; after he fails to reform, to repent, thunder is heard and he is swallowed up by the forces of Hell. After the smoke on the stage has cleared, the remaining characters in the drama sing a very pretty little sextet about how splendid it is that Don Giovanni has been destroyed, while they are alive and happy, and propose to seek a perfectly peaceful and contented and ordinary life, each in his own fashion: Mazzetto is going to marry Zerlina, Elvira will go back to her convent, Leporello will find a new master, Ottavio will marry Donna Anna, and so on. In the nineteenth century this perfectly harmless sextet, which is one of the most charming of Mozart's pieces, was regarded by the public as blasphemous, and was therefore never performed. It was first re-introduced into the European repertories, so far as I know, by Mahler, towards the end of the nineteenth or at the beginning of the twentieth century, and is now regularly played.

The reason is this. Here is this vast, dominating, sinister symbolic figure, Don Giovanni, who stands we know not for what, but certainly for something inexpressible. He stands, perhaps, for art as against life, for some principle of inexhaustible evil against some kind of philistine good; he stands for power, for magic, for some sort of infernal forces of a superhuman kind. The opera ends with an enormous climax, in which one infernal force is swallowed by another, and the vast melodrama rises to a volcanic culmination, which was meant to cow the audience, and to show them amidst what an unstable and terrifying world they lived; and then suddenly this philistine little sextet follows, in which the characters simply sing peacefully about the fact that a rake has been punished, and good men will continue their ordinary, perfectly peaceful lives thereafter. This was regarded as inartistic, shallow, bathetic and disgusting, and therefore eliminated.

This elevation of *Don Giovanni* into a vast myth, which dominates over us and which must be interpreted so as to convey the profoundest and most inexpressible aspects of the terrifying nature of reality, was certainly very far from the thoughts of the librettist, probably very far from the thoughts of Mozart. The librettist Lorenzo da Ponte, who started life as a converted Jew in

Venice, and ended it as a teacher of Italian in New York, was very remote from any thought of placing upon the stage one of the vast symbols of spiritual existence on earth. But in the nineteenth century this was the attitude taken towards Don Giovanni, who continued to haunt people's minds – he haunted Kierkegaard's mind to a very profound degree – and indeed does so until the present day. This is a very typical example of the total reversal of values, of the complete transformation of something which started off by being dry, classical, symmetrical, and in every respect in accordance with the conventions of the age; it had burst its frame, and suddenly began to spread its wings in the most unaccustomed and fearful fashion.

This view of great images dominating mankind – of dark forces, of the unconscious, of the importance of the inexpressible and the necessity of discounting it and allowing for it – spreads into every sphere of human activity, and is by no means confined to art. It enters, for example, into politics, first in a mild way, in Burke's great images of the great society of the dead and the living, and those not yet born, bound together by myriad unanalysable strands to which we are loyal, so that every attempt to try to analyse it rationally – say as a social contract or as some kind of utilitarian arrangement for the purpose of living a happier life, or preventing collisions with human beings – is shallow and betrays the inner, inexpressible spirit which dominates any human association, which carries it forward, loyalty to which, spiritual immersion in which, is at the very heart of true, genuine, deep, devoted human life. In Adam Müller, a German disciple of Burke, it reaches its most eloquent form. Science, he says, can reproduce only a lifeless political State; death cannot represent life, nor can stagnation (that is, the social contract, the liberal State, the English State in particular) represent movement. Science, utilitarianism, the use of machinery do not convey the State, which 'is not a mere factory, farm, insurance company or mercantile society; *it is the intimate binding together of the entire physical and spiritual needs of a nation, of its entire physical and spiritual riches, of its entire internal and external life, into a great energetic, infinitely active and living whole.*'

These mystical words then become the heart and centre of the whole organic theory of political life, and of loyalty to the State, and of the State as a semi-spiritual organisation, symbolic of the spiritual powers of divine mystery, which is undoubtedly what the State among the romantics, at least the more extreme romantics, becomes.

The same view enters the sphere of law. In the German school of historical jurisprudence true law is not that which a given authority, a king or an assembly, happens to pass; that is simply an empirical event, guided perhaps by utilitarian or other contemptible considerations. It is not that, nor is it something eternal – those laws of nature, those divine laws, which any rational soul can discover for itself, as taught by the Roman Church or by the Stoics or by the eighteenth-century French *philosophes*. These authorities may have disagreed about what these laws were or about how to discover them, but they all agreed that there were certain eternal, immutable principles on which human life had to be founded, and adherence to which made men moral, just and good. This is denied. Law is the product of the beating force within the nation, of dark traditional forces, of its organic sap which flows through its body as through a tree, of something which we cannot identify and cannot analyse, but which everyone who is true to his country feels coursing through his veins. Law is a traditional growth, partly a matter of circumstances, but partly the inner soul of the nation, now beginning to be conceived as almost individual – that which between them the members of the nation generate. True law is traditional law: every nation has its own law, every nation has its own shape; this shape goes far into the misty past, its roots are somewhere in the darkness, and unless its roots are in the darkness it is too easily overthrown. Joseph de Maistre, a reactionary French Catholic philosopher, who only half believed in this organic view of life, inasmuch as, theoretically at least, he was an adherent of Thomism, says that anything which man can make, man can mar. Anything which man can create, man can destroy; therefore the only thing which is eternal is this mysterious, frightening process which goes on far below the level of consciousness; this is what creates traditions, this is what creates States, nations, constitutions; anything written, anything articulated, anything arrived at by sensible men in a cool hour is a thin superficial thing, likely to collapse when other equally sane, equally superficial, equally reasonable men refute it – and it therefore has no true basis in reality.

This is also true of historical theories. The great German historical school tries to trace historical evolution in terms of unconscious dark factors interweaving with each other in all kinds of inexplicable ways. There is even such a thing as romantic economics, particularly in Germany, in the form, for example, of the economics of men like Fichte and Friedrich List, who believed in the necessity of creating an isolated State, *der geschlossene Handelsstaat*, in which the true spiritual force of the nation can exercise itself without being buffeted by other nations; that is to say, where the purpose of economics, the purpose of money and trade, is the spiritual self-perfection of man, and does not obey the so-called unbreakable laws of economics, as even people like Burke believed. Burke believed, indeed said, that the laws of commerce are the laws of nature, and therefore the laws of God, and deduced from this that nothing could be done about passing any radical reform, and the poor would have to starve – this is approximately the consequence of such a view. This was one of the consequences which brought the *laissez-faire* school of economics into a certain amount of justified disrepute. Romantic economics is the precise opposite of this. All economic institutions must be bent towards some kind of ideal of living together in a spiritually progressive manner. Above all you must not make the mistake of supposing that there are external laws, that there are objective, given laws of economics which are beyond human control. This is a typical return to the *rerum natura*. This means, once again, that you believe in a structure of things which can be studied, which sits still while you look at it and describe it – and this is false. Any such assumption that there are objective laws is simply a human fantasy, a human invention, an attempt on the part of human beings to justify their conduct, particularly their disreputable conduct, by calling into being, and placing responsibility upon the shoulders of, imaginary external laws, such as the laws of supply and demand, or any other kind of external law – this law of politics, that law of economics – which is alleged to be unalterable, and which therefore not only explains but justifies poverty, squalor and other unattractive social phenomena.

In this respect the romantics could be either progressive or reactionary. In what might be called the revolutionary States, the radical States created after the French Revolution, they were reactionary, they called for the return of some kind of medieval darkness; in reactionary States, such as Prussia after 1812, they became progressive, inasmuch as they regarded this creation of the King of Prussia as a suffocating, artificial mechanism which stifled the natural organic thrust of the life of the human beings imprisoned by it. It could take either form. That is why we encounter revolutionary romantics and reactionary romantics. That is why it is impossible to pin romanticism down to any given political view, however often this has been tried.

Those are the fundamental bases of romanticism: will, the fact that there is no structure to things, that you can mould things as you will – they come into being only as a result of your moulding activity – and therefore opposition to any view which tried to represent reality as having some kind of form which could be studied, written down, learnt, communicated to others, and in other respects treated in a scientific manner.

There is no province in which this attitude is more evident than the field of music, about which I have not yet had anything to say. It is interesting and, indeed, even amusing to watch the development of attitudes towards music from the beginning of the eighteenth to the middle of the nineteenth century. In the eighteenth century, particularly in France, music is regarded as a fairly inferior art. Vocal music has its place because it heightens the importance of the words, religious music has its place because it contributes to the mood which religion is meant to induce. Even earlier, d'Urfé says that it is obvious that visual art is far more sensitive to the spiritual life of man than the ear. Fontenelle, the most civilised man of his time, and indeed of most times, said, when instrumental music first began to invade France, and sonatas began to appear, as against the kind of vocal religious music or operatic music to which he was used, which had a plot, which had an explanation, which had some kind of extra-musical importance: 'Sonate, que me veux-tu?' – 'Sonata, what do you want of me?' –

and condemned instrumental music as a meaningless pattern of sounds, not really suitable for delicate or civilised ears.

This is a fairly common attitude in France in the middle of the eighteenth century. It comes out with particular vividness in the verses addressed by the essayist and dramatist Marmontel in the 1770s to the composer Gluck, who at this period conquered the Paris stage. Gluck, as everyone knows, reformed music by placing music above the words, and by forcing the words into some conformity with the true emotion and drama which he wished to convey by means of the music – the great musical reform of no longer using music as a mere accompaniment to the meaning of the actual dramatic words. This outraged Marmontel, who supposed drama and all art to have some kind of mimetic quality, that its function was imitation of life, imitation of the ideals of life, imitation of imaginary beings, ideal beings, not necessarily real beings, but still some kind of imitation, some kind of relationship to actual events, actual persons, actual emotions, something which was there in reality, which it was the business of the artist if necessary to idealise, but at any rate to represent as it truly is. Music, which had no meaning by itself – it was simply a succession of sounds – was clearly non-mimetic. Everybody saw that. Words had something to do with the words spoken in ordinary life, paints had something to do with colours perceived in nature, but sounds were very dissimilar to the sounds heard in rustling forests, or to birdsong. The kinds of sounds which musicians used were clearly much remoter from any kind of ordinary human experience than were the materials used by other artists. Hence Marmontel attacked Gluck in the following words:

> Il arriva le jongleur de Bohême.
> Il arriva précédé de son nom;
> Sur le débris d'un superbe poème,
> Il fit beugler Achille, Agamemnon;
> Il fit hurler la reine Clytemnestre;
> Il fit ronfler l'infatigable orchestre;

[He has arrived, the mountebank from Bohemia, he has arrived, preceded by his reputation. Upon the ruins of a superb poem he makes

Achilles and Agamemnon howl, he makes Queen Clytemnestra scream, he makes the indefatigable orchestra roar.]

This is a very typical attack of its time. It is the attitude of those who did not wish to give up association with nature, or the idea of imitation, to this peculiar notion of mere expression of the inner soul. This is true of Fontanes, writing in 1785. For him, the only purpose of music is to evoke certain emotions; unless it evokes some kind of emotion which is already there, unless it is reminiscent of something, unless it is associated with experience of some kind, it has no value. Sounds as such express nothing and need never be employed in this way. Madame de Staël very typically, already at the beginning of the nineteenth century, speaking about music, of which she alleged herself to be extremely fond, said something of this sort about where the value of music lies. 'What man,' she says, 'exhausted by a life of passion, can listen with indifference to the tune which enlivened the dances and games of his tranquil youth? What woman whose beauty time has at last ravaged can hear without emotion the song that her lover once sang?' No doubt this is true, but this is a very different type of approach to music from that which was already being expressed by the romantic Germans of this period. Even Stendhal, who liked Rossini with an almost physical passion, says about the music of Beethoven that he detests the combinations of this learned and almost mathematical harmony – rather the sort of thing which people nowadays might be inclined to say about Schoenberg.

This is very different from Wackenroder, who wrote in the 1790s that music 'shows us all the movements of our spirit, disembodied', or from Schopenhauer, who says, 'The composer reveals to us the intimate essence of the world; he is the interpreter of the profoundest wisdom, speaking a language which reason cannot understand.' Neither reason, nor indeed anything else: that is Schopenhauer's point, because he saw music as the expression of the naked will, of that internal energy which moves the world, of that inexpressible inner drive which is the essence, for him, of reality, and which all other arts to some extent try to tame, order, arrange, organise and to that extent cut into, distort and kill. This is also the view of Tieck and of August Wilhelm Schlegel, indeed of all the romantics, some of whom were very fond of music. There are remarkable essays by Hoffmann not only on Beethoven and on Mozart, but also on the actual cosmic, metaphysical significance of, for example, the tonic and the fifth, which are described as vast giants in glittering arms. He also has a little essay on the true significance of a particular key, say the key of A flat minor, which at that period is a very unlikely thing to have been written about by a member of any other European nation.

Music, then, is seen as abstract, detached from life, a form of direct expression, non-mimetic, non-imitative, and at the furthest possible remove from any kind of objective description of anything. Nevertheless, the romantics did not think that the arts ought to be unbridled, that one should simply sing whatever comes into one's head, paint whatever one's mood orders one to paint, or give completely undisciplined expression to the emotions – they have been charged with this by Irving Babbitt and others, but mistakenly. Novalis says very clearly, 'When storms rage in the poet's breast, and he is bewildered and confused, gibberish results.' A poet must not wander idly all day in search of feelings and images. Certainly he must have these feelings and images, plainly he must allow these storms to rage – for how indeed can he avoid it? – but then he must discipline them, then he must find the proper medium for their expression. Schubert said that the mark of a great composer is to be caught in a vast battle of inspiration, in which the forces rage in the most uncontrolled way, but to keep one's head in the course of this storm and direct the troops. This is quite clearly a far more genuine expression of what artists do than the remarks of the more unbridled romantics, who were unaware of the nature of art inasmuch as they were not artists themselves.

Who were these persons who so celebrated the will, who so hated the fixed nature of reality, and who believed in these storms, these untamable, these unbridgeable abysses, these unorganisable streams? It is very difficult to give any sociological explanation for the rise of the romantic movement, although it ought to be done. The only explanation I have ever been able to discover arises from looking at who these persons were, particularly in Germany. The truth is that they were a remarkably unworldly body of men. They were poor, they were timid, they were bookish, they were very awkward in society. They were easily snubbed, they had to serve as tutors to great men, they were constantly full of insult and oppression. It is clear that they were confined and contracted in their universe; they were like Schiller's bent twig, which always jumped back and hit its bender. There was something about Prussia, where most of them came from – about this excessively paternalistic State of Frederick the Great's, about the fact that he was a mercantilist and therefore increased the wealth of Prussia, increased her army, made her the most powerful and rich of all the German States, but at the same time pauperised her peasants and did not allow sufficient opportunity to most of her citizens. It is true, too, that these men, most of them children of clergymen and of civil servants and the like, received an education which gave them certain intellectual and emotional ambitions; with the result that, since too many jobs in Prussia were held by persons of good birth, where social distinctions were preserved in the most rigorous manner, they were not able to attain full expression of their ambitions, and therefore did become somewhat frustrated, and began to breed fantasies of every possible kind.

There is something in this. At any rate, it seems to me to be a more reasonable explanation – that men of a humiliated kind, excited by the French Revolution and by the general overturn of events, should have given rise to this movement – than the theory of Louis Hautecoeur, who thinks that the movement began in France, among ladies, and is due to the effect upon the nerves of the consumption of too much tea and coffee, of corsets which were too tight, of cosmetics which were poisonous and of other means of self-beautification which had physically deleterious results. This does not appear to me, on the whole, a theory which is worth pursuing very much further.

At any rate, the movement arose in Germany, and there it found its truest home. But it travelled beyond the confines of Germany to every country where there was some kind of social discontent and dissatisfaction, particularly to countries oppressed by small élites of brutal or oppressive or inefficient men, especially in Eastern Europe. Perhaps it found its most passionate expression in, of all countries, England, where Byron was the leader of the entire romantic movement, in the sense that Byronism became almost synonymous with romanticism in the early nineteenth century.

How Byron became a romantic is too long a story, which I do not think I could attempt to tell even if I knew it. But there is no doubt that he was a kind of person perhaps best described by Chateaubriand, who said: 'The Ancients scarcely knew this secret anxiety, the bitterness of strangled passions, all fermenting together. A large political life, games in the gymnasium or on the field of Mars, the business of the Forum – public business – filled their time and left no place for the ennui of the heart.' That was certainly Byron's condition, and Chateaubriand, who was perhaps only half a romantic, a romantic only in the sense that he was subjective and introspective and tried to make a kind of vague myth out of Christian values to replace the no longer available myths of the ancient world and the Middle Ages, described it accurately.

Chateaubriand is half respectful and half ironical towards this movement. Perhaps the best expression of it was given by a little French jingle, written by an anonymous poet in the middle of the nineteenth century:

> L'obéissance est douce au vil coeur des classiques;
> Ils ont toujours quelqu'un pour modèle et pour loi.
> Un artiste ne doit écouter que son moi,
> Et l'orgueil seul emplit les âmes romantiques.

[Obedience is sweet to the vile heart of the classics: they always have someone as a model or as a law. An artist must listen only to his own self, and pride alone fills romantic souls.]

This is certainly the position of Byron in the emotional, and indeed political, world of the nineteenth century. Byron's chief emphasis is upon the indomitable will, and the whole philosophy of voluntarism, the whole philosophy of the view that there is a world which must be subdued and subjugated by superior persons, takes its rise from him. The French romantics from Hugo onwards are disciples of Byron. Byron and Goethe are the great names, but Goethe was a very ambiguous romantic, and although in Faust he created somebody who keeps saying 'Forward, forward, never stop, never cease, never ask the moment to wait; over murder, over crime, over every conceivable obstacle the romantic spirit must forge its way', his later works and his life belied it. Byron acted out his beliefs in the most convincing fashion. Here are some typical lines of his which entered into European consciousness and infected the entire romantic movement:

> Apart he stalked in joyless reverie . . .
> With pleasure drugged, he almost longed for woe,
> And e'en for change of scene would seek the shades below.[1]

> There was in him a vital scorn of all . . .
> He stood a stranger in this breathing world . . .
> So much he soared beyond, or sunk beneath,
> The men with whom he felt condemned to breathe . . .

This is the typical note of the outcast, the exile, the superman, the man who cannot put up with the existing world because his soul is too large to contain it, because he has ideals which presuppose the necessity for perpetual fervent movement forward, movement which is constantly confined by the stupidity and the unimaginativeness and the flatness of the existing world. Therefore the lives of Byronic figures begin in scorn, pass into vice, and from there to crime, to terror and to despair. That is the ordinary career of all the Giaours and Laras and Cains who fill his poetry. Here is Manfred:

> My Spirit walked not with the souls of men,
> Nor looked upon the earth with human eyes;
> The thirst of their ambition was not mine,
> The aim of their existence was not mine;
> My joys – my griefs – my passions – and my powers,
> Made me a stranger . . .

The whole of the Byronic syndrome consists in adhesion to the two values which I have tried to expound, the will and the absence of a structure of the world to which one must adjust oneself. From

[1] By 'the shades below' he means death.

Byron the syndrome passes to others, to Lamartine, to Victor Hugo, to Nodier, to the French romantics in general; from them it goes further, to Schopenhauer, who sees man as being tossed in a kind of frail bark upon a vast ocean of the will, which has no purpose, no end, no direction, which man can resist only at his own peril, with which man can come to terms only if he manages to rid himself of this unnecessary desire to order, to tidy himself up, to create a cosy home for himself in this wild and unpredictable element. From Schopenhauer it goes on to Wagner, whose whole sermon in *The Ring*, for example, is the appalling nature of unsatisfiable desire, which must lead to the most fearful suffering and ultimately to the immolation in the most violent fashion of all those who are possessed by a desire which they can at one and the same time neither avoid nor satisfy. The result of this must be some kind of ultimate extinction: the waters of the Rhine rise and cover this violent, this chaotic, this unstoppable, this incurable disease by which all mortals are affected. That is the heart of the romantic movement in Europe.

Let me now go back and consider again what the position is with regard to that long catalogue which I gave at the outset. I tried to show that romanticism appeared on the surface to say everything and its opposite. If I am right, then perhaps it is possible to maintain that these two principles, the necessity of the will and the absence of a structure of things, may satisfy most of the criteria I mentioned, and that the contradictions which appeared so stringent are not perhaps quite so violent as they may seem.

To begin with what Lovejoy complained about so bitterly: How can it be that the word 'romanticism' stands at one and the same time for two such contradictory things as, on the one hand, noble savages, primitivism, the simple life, rosy-cheeked peasants, a turning away from the frightful sophistication of the cities and towards the then smiling prairies of the United States, or some other simple form of life in some real or imaginary part of the globe; and on the other hand blue wigs, green hair, absinthe and Gérard de Nerval pulling his lobster along the streets of Paris in order to attract some degree of attention to himself, which indeed he succeeded in doing? If you ask what is common to these two – and Lovejoy quite naturally expresses a certain surprise that the same word should be comfortably used for both – the answer is that they both wish to break up the nature of the given. In the eighteenth century you have an extreme order of sophistication, you have forms, you have rules, you have laws, you have etiquette, you have an extremely tight and well-organised form of life, whether in the arts or in politics or in any other sphere. Anything which destroys this, anything which blows it up, is welcome. Therefore whether you go to the Isles of the Blest, whether you go to the noble Indians, whether you go to the simple uncorrupted heart of the simple man, as sung of by Rousseau, on the one hand; or whether on the other hand you go to green wigs and blue waistcoats and men of wild distempers and people of the most extreme sophistication and savage bohemianism of life; whichever of these you go to, at any rate both are methods of blowing up, of shattering, that which is given. When in Hoffmann brass knockers become old women, or old women become city councillors, or city councillors become bowls of punch, this is not meant simply to titillate your feelings, not meant simply to be a slightly fantastic kind of story which gives pleasure and is immediately forgotten; when in Gogol's famous story 'The Nose' a nose detaches itself from the face of a minor civil servant and then has romantic adventures of a very violent kind in a top hat and a greatcoat, this is not meant merely to be a rather peculiar story, but to be an invasion of, an attack upon, the hideous nature of the unalterable given. There is a wish to show that underneath this smooth surface there are frightful inexpressible forces boiling, that nothing can be taken for granted, and that a profound view of life essentially entails the breaking of this mirror-like surface. Whichever way you turn, whether it is towards extreme sophistication or some unheard of simplicity, the result is the same.

Of course, if you think that you can actually become a noble savage, if you think that you can actually transform yourself into a simple native of some unsophisticated country, living a very primitive life, then the magic is gone. But none of them did. The whole point of the romantic vision of the noble savage was that he was unattainable. If he had been attainable, he would have been useless, because then he would have become an awful given, a frightful rule of life, just as confining, just as disciplining, just as detestable as that which it replaced. Therefore it is the unfindable, the unattainable, the infinite which are the heart of the matter.

Similarly, what is it that is common to, on the one hand, the enchanters and the phantoms and the griffins and the moats and the ghosts, and the gibbering bats which surround medieval castles, and the ghosts of bloody hands and the fearful dark voices which reach you from all kinds of mysterious and terrifying ravines – what is there common to these and, on the other hand, the great spectacle of the peaceful, organic medieval era, with its tournaments, its heralds and its priests, its royal personages and its aristocracy, quiet, dignified, unalterable and essentially at peace with itself? (Both kinds of phenomena are the stock-in-trade of romantic writers.) The answer is that both, if placed alongside the daily reality of an early industrial civilisation, in Lyons or in Birmingham, compromise it.

Take the extraordinary case of Scott. Here is a writer commonly accounted a romantic. It may be asked, as indeed a number of puzzled Marxist critics do ask: Why is Scott a romantic author? Scott is simply an extremely imaginative and scrupulous writer who managed to describe with considerable fidelity, in a way that affected all kinds of historians, the life of ages preceding his own – say seventeenth-century Scotland, or thirteenth-century England, or fifteenth-century France. Why is this romantic? By itself it would not be. Naturally if you are simply a very faithful and scrupulous medieval historian describing the exact customs of your ancestors, you are just being a historian in the best classical tradition. You are merely telling the truth as well as you are able, and this is in no sense romantic, but on the contrary a highly reputable academic activity. But Scott was a romantic writer. Why was this? Simply because he liked these forms of life? That is not quite enough. The point is that by painting these very attractive and delightful and hypnotic pictures of these ages he placed alongside our values – by which I mean the values of 1810, the values of 1820, the values of his own contemporary Scotland, or his own contemporary England or France, which were what they were, the values of the early nineteenth century – by the side of these values, whatever they may have been, Protestant, unromantic, industrial, at any rate not medieval, he placed another set of values, equally good if not better, in competition with them. This shattered the monopoly, shattered the possibility that every age is as good as it can be, and is indeed advancing to an even better one.

If you look for the difference between Macaulay and Scott, you will find it precisely in this, that Macaulay really does believe in progress. He believes everything fits into its own place and that the seventeenth century was less fortunate than the eighteenth, and the eighteenth much less lucky than the nineteenth. Everything is all right where it is. Everything can be explained in terms of its own causal forces. We are progressing. Everything fits, everything advances; at a certain cost, it may be, but at the same time if it were not for human stupidity, human idleness, human perversity and other dark forces, vested interests and the like, we should be progressing much faster. This he had in common, to some degree, with James Mill and the Utilitarians. With Bacon, he did not believe in mystical religion, that is plain. This is a picture whereby you say there is a reality, it has a certain nature, we study it, we are scientific, we know more now than we used to know before. Our ancestors did not know how to become happy, we know it better. We do not know it perfectly, but we know it better, and our descendants will know it better still. Whether we ever get to the goal of a perfect society, stable, unalterable, with all possible and actual human wishes totally satisfied in a harmonious manner, nobody can tell, but it is not an absurd ideal. This is the ideal of the jigsaw puzzle solved.

If Scott is right, this cannot be true. This is like Herder again. If there are values in the past which are more valuable than those of the present, or at least in competition with them, if there is a magnificent civilisation somewhere in thirteenth-century Britain or in some remote part of the world, whether in space or in time, which is as attractive as, if not more so than, the drab civilisation in which you are living, but nevertheless (and that is the important thing) irreproducible – you cannot get back to it, it cannot be rebuilt, it must remain a dream, it must remain a fantasy, it must remain an object of disappointment if you seek it – if that is so, then nothing will satisfy you, because two ideals have come into collision and it is impossible to solve the collision. It is impossible to obtain a state of affairs which will contain the best of all these cultures, because they are not compatible. Therefore the notion of incompatibility, of plurality of ideals, each of which has its own validity, becomes part of the great battering-ram which romanticism employs against the notion of order, against the notion of progress, against the notion of perfection, classical ideals, the structure of things. That is why Scott, surprisingly enough, is correctly called a romantic writer.

No universal pattern, no great style: *la ligne vraie* of which Diderot spoke, the real line, the underground tradition to which T. S. Eliot wished to penetrate – these are the things which are denied and denounced by the entire romantic movement from the beginning to the end as a fearful delusion, likely to lead only to stupidity and shallowness on the part of those who pursue it. This is Pope's '*Nature Methodiz'd*', this is Aristotle, this is what the romantics most bitterly detested. Therefore one must break up this order: one must break it up by going to the past, or by going within oneself and out of the external world. One must go and seek to be one with some kind of great spiritual drive with which one will never completely identify oneself, or one must idealise some myth which will never quite come to pass, the Nordic myth or the Southern myth or a Celtic myth or some other myth, it does not matter which – class or nation or Church or whatever it may be – which will constantly drive you forward, which will never be fulfilled, the essence and value of which is that it is strictly unfulfillable, so that if it were fulfilled it would be worthless. That is the essence of the romantic movement, so far as I can see: will, and man as an activity, as something which cannot be described because it is perpetually creating; you must not even say that it is creating itself, for there is no self, there is only movement. That is the heart of romanticism.

Finally, something ought to be said about the consequences of romanticism in the present day. It has certainly had consequences, to a very vast degree, though it was met by certain counter-forces which to some extent softened the blow.

There is no doubt, whatever else may be said about romanticism, that it did put its finger upon something which classicism had left out, upon these unconscious dark forces, upon the fact that the classical description of men, and the description of men by scientists or scientifically influenced men such as Helvétius or James Mill or H. G. Wells or Shaw or Russell – does not capture the whole of man. It recognised that there were certain aspects of human existence, particularly the inward aspects of human life, which were totally left out, so that the picture was distorted in a very violent degree. One of the movements which it led to in the present is the so-called existentialist movement in France, about which I should like to say a few words; for existentialism seems to me the truest heir of romanticism.

The great achievement of romanticism, that which I took as my starting-point, was that, unlike most other great movements in human history, it succeeded in transforming certain of our values to a very profound degree. That is what made existentialism possible. First I shall say something about these values, and then I shall attempt to show how romanticism penetrates this modern philosophy, and how it enters into certain other phenomena of modern life as well, such as the emotive theory of ethics and Fascism, each of which it has profoundly influenced.

I have indicated already – but I must now put greater stress on the fact – that a new cluster of virtues appeared with the romantic movement. Since we are wills, and since we must be free in the Kantian or Fichtean sense, motive counts more than consequence. For consequences cannot be controlled, but motives can. Since we must be free, and since we must be ourselves to the fullest possible degree, the great virtue – the greatest virtue of all – is what existentialists call authenticity, and what the romantics called sincerity. As I tried to say before, this is new: I do not believe that in the seventeenth century, if you had a religious conflict between a Protestant and a Catholic, it would have been possible for the Catholic to say, 'The Protestant is a damnable heretic and leads souls to perdition, but the fact that he is sincere raises him in my estimation. The fact that he is sincere, that he's prepared to lay down his life for the nonsense in which he believes, is a morally noble fact. Anyone who is sufficiently a man of integrity, anyone who is prepared to sacrifice himself upon any altar, no matter what, has a moral personality which is worthy of respect, no matter how detestable or how false the ideals to which he bows his knee.' The notion of idealism is new. Idealism means that you respect people for being prepared to give up health, wealth, popularity, power, all kinds of desirable things which their emotions demand, to relinquish that which they cannot control themselves, what Kant called the external factors, emotions which are themselves part of the psychological or physical world, to lay that aside for the sake of something with which they truly identify themselves, no matter what. The notion that idealism is a good thing and realism a bad one – that if I say I am something of a realist I mean I am about to tell a lie or do something peculiarly shabby – is the result of the romantic movement. Sincerity becomes a virtue in itself.

This is at the heart of the whole thing. The fact that there is admiration, from the 1820s onwards, for minorities as such, for defiance as such, for failure as being nobler in certain respects than success, for every kind of opposition to reality, for taking up positions on principle where the principle may itself be absurd; the fact that this is not regarded with the kind of contempt with which you regard a man who says twice 2 is 7, which is also a principle, but which nevertheless you know to be the assertion of something false – this is significant. What romanticism did was to undermine the notion that in matters of value, politics, morals, aesthetics there are such things as objective criteria which operate between human beings, such that anyone who does not use these criteria is simply either a liar or a madman, which is true of mathematics or of physics. This division between where objective truth obtains – in mathematics, in physics, in certain regions of common sense – and where objective truth has been compromised – in ethics, in aesthetics and the rest – is new, and has created a new attitude to life – whether good or bad, I shall not volunteer to say.

This comes out if we ask ourselves what kind of moral evaluation we should make of certain historical personages. In the first place we might look at utilitarian figures, so to speak, who conferred benefits upon mankind, such as Frederick the Great or Kemal Pasha, about whom we might think that their private characters were not irreproachable, of whom we might say that they were perhaps in certain respects hard-hearted or brutal or cruel, or not at all free from certain impulses which, on the whole, human beings disapprove of. At the same time there is no doubt that they improved the lives of their peoples, they were competent, they were efficient, they raised the level of life, they created great organisations which have lasted, and they have been the source of a great deal of satisfaction, strength and happiness to a large number of persons. Now suppose that we compare these with someone who obviously caused suffering, such as John of Leiden, who caused cannibalism to occur in the city of Münster, who caused a large number of people to be slaughtered for the sake of his own apocalyptic religion, or Torquemada, who destroyed a very large number of persons whom today we should consider innocent for the sake of their souls, for the purest possible motive. Which of these persons should be rated higher? In the eighteenth century there would have been no doubt. Frederick the Great clearly comes above a religious madman. Today, however, people would suffer from certain doubts, because they think that idealism, sincerity, dedication, purity of heart, purity of mind are qualities preferable to corruption, wickedness, calculation, egoism, mendacity, the desire to exploit other people for one's own benefit, of which these great State-founders were undoubtedly guilty.

Therefore we are children of both worlds. On the one hand we are heirs to romanticism, because romanticism broke that great single mould in which humanity in one way or another had marched hitherto, the *philosophia perennis*. We are products of certain doubts – we cannot quite tell. We give so many marks for consequence, so many marks for motive, and we oscillate between the two. If it goes too far, if someone is a Hitler, then we do not think that his sincerity is necessarily a saving quality, although in the 1930s it was much argued in his favour. He must go very far indeed, but if he does he flouts values which are of an extremely universal kind. So that we are still members of some kind of unified tradition, but the field within which we now oscillate freely, the amount of allowance we make, is far greater than it has ever been before. For this the romantic movement is to a great degree responsible, inasmuch as it preached the incompatibility of ideals, the importance of motive, the importance of character, or at any rate of purpose, over consequence, over efficiency, over effect, over happiness, success and position in the world. Happiness is not an ideal, said Hölderlin, happiness is 'tepid water on the tongue';

Nietzsche said 'Man does not desire happiness, only the English-man does.' Sentiments of this kind would have been laughed at in the seventeenth or eighteenth centuries. If they are not laughed at now, this is perhaps the direct product of the romantic movement.

The central sermon of existentialism is essentially a romantic one, namely, that there is in the world nothing to lean on. Suppose you try to explain your conduct, and you say 'C'est plus fort que moi', it is too strong for me, emotion overcame me; or, there are certain principles of an objective kind which, although I hate them, I must subserve; or, I have received orders from an institution which is eternal or divine, or which is of an objectively valid character, and although I may not like this, it has given the order – 'it' being the laws of economics, or the Ministry of the Interior, or whatever it may be – and it has a right to my obedience. Once you begin doing this you are simply using alibis. You are simply pretending that you are not deciding, when you have in reality decided but do not care to face the consequences of the fact that it is you who have decided.

Even when you say: I am partly unconscious, I am the product of unconscious forces, I cannot help it, I have a complex, it is not my fault, I am driven, it is because my father was unkind to my mother that I am today the monster that I am – this, according to existentialism (which is probably right on this point), is an attempt to curry favour or to obtain sympathy by transferring the weight of responsibility for your acts, in performing which you are entirely free, to something objective – it does not matter whether it is a political organisation or a psychological doctrine. You are trying to shift responsibility from your shoulders (because it is you who make the decision) somewhere else. Once you say that you are a monster – and do not mind being a monster, evidently – this is a kind of complacent acceptance of something which you know to be evil, but from which you remove the curse by saying: not I, society is responsible; we are all determined, we cannot help it, there is a causality which pervades the world, and I am merely the instrument of powerful forces which I can no more prevent from making me evil than I can prevent them from making you good; you are not to be congratulated for being good, nor am I to be condemned for being evil; we can neither of us help our fate; we are simply fragments of an enormous causal process.

Sartre, with a certain justice, echoes the views of Fichte, echoes the views of Kant, from whom all this comes, ultimately, in saying that this is either self-deception or deliberate deception of others. The existentialists go further than this. They reject the very notion of a metaphysical structure of the universe, the very notion of theology or metaphysics, the attempt to say that certain things have essences (which merely means that things are what they are of necessity), that we arrive in a world which has a certain structure that cannot be altered – a physical structure, chemical structure, social structure, psychological structure, and a metaphysical and a theological structure, with God at the head of this great creation and the amoeba below, or whatever it is you may believe in. These are nothing but pathetic attempts on the part of human beings to make themselves at home in the world by breeding enormous cosy fantasies, to see the world in such a way that they can fit into it more comfortably and do not have to face the appalling prospect of taking upon their own shoulders total responsibility for all their acts. When they give reasons for doing what they do, when they say, 'I have done this because of that, in order to pursue this', and you say 'But why should you pursue this particular end?' and they say 'Because it is objectively right', that too for the existentialist is an attempt to transfer responsibility for what should be free choice in a vacuum on to something which is not yours, which is objective – natural law, the sayings of the sages, the pronouncements of sacred books, the pronouncements of scientists in a laboratory, what psychologists and sociologists say, what politicians or economists declare – not I, they. This is regarded as an attempt to shuffle off responsibility and to blind oneself, unnecessarily, to the fact that the universe is in reality a kind of void – that is what is meant by calling it absurd – in which you and you alone exist, and you make whatever there is to make, and you are responsible for making what you make, and you cannot plead extenuation. All excuses are false and all explanations are explainings away; and this might as well be faced by a man who is brave enough and tragic enough to face reality as he should. This is the stoic sermon of existentialism and it derives directly from romanticism.

Some romantics certainly went too far. This can be illustrated by the extraordinary example of Max Stirner, which may perhaps show what it is, in the end, that is valuable in romanticism, even for us today. Stirner was a Hegelian German schoolmaster who argued, quite correctly, as follows. The romantics are quite right in supposing that when we think that institutions are eternal this is a mistake. Institutions are created freely by human beings for the benefit of other human beings and in time become worn out. When therefore, by looking at them from the point of view of the present, we see they are worn out, we must abolish them and have new institutions, freely arrived at by our own indomitable will. This is not merely true of political institutions, economic institutions or other public institutions; it is equally true of doctrines. Doctrines can also be a most terrible weight upon us, fearful chains and tyrannies which yoke us to all kinds of views which the present or our own wills no longer desiderate. Therefore theories, too, must be blown up; any kind of general theory – Hegelianism, Marxism – is itself a ghastly form of despotism which claims to have some kind of objective validity beyond the choice of individual men. This cannot be right, for it confines us and cribs us and limits our free activity. But if this is true about doctrines, it will be equally true of all general propositions; and if it is true of all general propositions, then – and this is the last step of all, which some romantics certainly took – it is true of all words, because all words are general, they all classify. If I use the word 'yellow' I want to mean by it what I meant by it yesterday and what you will mean by it tomorrow. But this is a terrible yoke, this is a fearful despotism. Why should the word 'yellow' mean the same thing now and tomorrow? Why cannot I alter it? Why should twice 2 always make 4? Why should words be uniform? Why cannot I make up my own universe each time I begin? But if I do that, if there is no systematic symbolism, then I cannot think. If I cannot think, I go mad.

To do him justice, Stirner did duly go mad. He ended his life very honourably and very consistently in a lunatic asylum as a perfectly peaceful harmless lunatic, in 1856.

Something of the sort was also boiling in the mind of Nietzsche, who was a far superior thinker, but who in certain respects resembles Stirner. From this a moral may be drawn, namely that so long as we live in society, we communicate. If we did not communicate we should hardly be men. Part of what we mean by 'human being' is that such a being should understand a portion, at any rate, of what we say to him. To this extent, then, there must be common language, common communication and, to some degree, common values, otherwise there will be no intelligibility between human beings. A human being who cannot understand what any other human being says is scarcely a human being; he is pronounced abnormal. To the extent to which there is normality, and communication, there are common values. To the extent to which there are common values, it is impossible to say that everything must be created by me; that if I find something given, I must smash it; that if I find something structured, I must destroy it in order to give free play to my unbridled imagination. To this extent romanticism, if it is driven to its logical conclusion, does end in some kind of lunacy.

Fascism too is an inheritor of romanticism, not because it is irrational – plenty of movements have been that – nor because of a belief in élites – plenty of movements have held that belief. The reason why Fascism owes something to romanticism is, again, because of the notion of the unpredictable will either of a man or of a group, which forges forward in some fashion that is impossible to organise, impossible to predict, impossible to rationalise. That is the whole heart of Fascism: what the leader will say tomorrow, how the spirit will move us, where we shall go, what we shall do – that cannot be foretold. The hysterical self-assertion and the nihilistic destruction of existing institutions because they confine the unlimited will, which is the only thing which counts for human beings; the superior person who crushes the inferior because his will is stronger; these are a direct inheritance – in an extremely distorted and garbled form, no doubt, but still an inheritance – from the romantic movement; and this inheritance has played an extremely powerful part in our lives.

The whole movement, indeed, is an attempt to impose an aesthetic model upon reality, to say that everything should obey the rules of art. For artists, indeed, perhaps some of the claims of romanticism may appear to have a great deal of validity. But their attempt to convert life into art presupposes that human beings are stuff, that they are simply a kind of material, even as paints or sounds are kinds of material: and to the degree to which this is not true, to the degree to which human beings, in order to communicate with each other, are forced to recognise certain common values, certain common facts, to live in a common world; to the extent to which not everything which science says is nonsense, not everything which common sense declares is untrue – because to say that is in itself a self-contradictory and absurd proposition – to this extent romanticism in its full form, and even its offshoots in the form of both existentialism and Fascism, seem to me to be fallacious.

What can we be said to owe to romanticism? A great deal. We owe to romanticism the notion of the freedom of the artist, and the fact that neither he nor human beings in general can be explained by oversimplified views such as were prevalent in the eighteenth century and such as are still enunciated by over-rational and over-scientific analysts either of human beings or of groups. We also owe to romanticism the notion that a unified answer in human affairs is likely to be ruinous, that if you really believe there is one single solution to all human ills, and that you must impose this solution at no matter what cost, you are likely to become a violent and despotic tyrant in the name of your solution, because your desire to remove all obstacles to it will end by destroying those creatures for whose benefit you offer the solution. The notion that there are many values, and that they are incompatible; the whole notion of plurality, of inexhaustibility, of the imperfection of all human answers and arrangements; the notion that no single answer which claims to be perfect and true, whether in art or in life, can in principle be perfect or true – all this we owe to the romantics.

As a result a rather peculiar situation has arisen. Here are the romantics, whose chief burden is to destroy ordinary tolerant life, to destroy philistinism, to destroy common sense, to destroy the peaceful avocations of men, to raise everybody to some passionate level of self-expressive experience, of such a kind as perhaps only divinities, in older works of literature, were supposed to manifest. This is the ostensible sermon, the ostensible purpose of romanticism, whether among the Germans or in Byron or among the

French, or whoever it may be; and yet, as a result of making clear the existence of a plurality of values, as a result of driving wedges into the notion of the classical ideal, of the single answer to all questions, of the rationalisability of everything, of the answerability of all questions, of the whole jigsaw-puzzle conception of life, they have given prominence to and laid emphasis upon the incompatibility of human ideals. But if these ideals are incompatible, then human beings sooner or later realise that they must make do, they must make compromises, because if they seek to destroy others, others will seek to destroy them; and so, as a result of this passionate, fanatical, half-mad doctrine, we arrive at an appreciation of the necessity of tolerating others, the necessity of preserving an imperfect equilibrium in human affairs, the impossibility of driving human beings so far into the pen which we have created for them, or into the single solution which possesses us, that they will ultimately revolt against us, or at any rate be crushed by it.

The result of romanticism, then, is liberalism, toleration, decency and the appreciation of the imperfections of life; some degree of increased rational self-understanding. This was very far from the intentions of the romantics. But at the same time – and to this extent the romantic doctrine is true – they are the persons who most strongly emphasised the unpredictability of all human activities. They were hoist with their own petard. Aiming at one thing, they produced, fortunately for us all, almost the exact opposite.

REFERENCES

... a cumbrous editorial apparatus apparently, if hopelessly,
designed to embalm the most effervescent of all contemporary
historians.

Nicholas Richardson[1]

One of the ways in which [*The Proper Study of Mankind*]
presents a slightly bastardised state of [Berlin's] essays is that
Henry Hardy has done his best to kit them out in full footnoted
fig; this is no doubt helpful for anyone wanting to trace one of
Berlin's references, but it does threaten to domesticate what had
been personal and stylish into appearing merely conventional and
industrious.

Stefan Collini[2]

It would not be difficult for a scholar with heavy teaching
commitments to devote the spare hours of his whole working life
to the edition and exegesis of one Greek play. As I am ...
inclined to think that a job half done today is more useful to
students of Greek literature than a promise that the job will be
finished tomorrow, I decided that I would finish work on *Clouds*
by a certain date, even if I knew that another year would produce
some improvements ...

Kenneth Dover[3]

THIS CUMBROUS epigraphic apparatus provides a useful background for the few introductory remarks I wish to make about the
notes on sources that follow.

---

[1] Reviewing Berlin's *Russian Thinkers* in *New Society*, 19 January 1978, p. 142.
[2] Reviewing Berlin's *The Proper Study of Mankind* in *The Times Literary Supplement*, 22 August 1997, p. 3.
[3] Preface to Aristophanes, *Clouds* (Oxford, 1968), p. v.

Stefan Collini is of course right that to add references in footnotes to a plain text is to commit an alteration of tone. However, it is an alteration of which Isaiah Berlin thoroughly approved; had it not been, I should not have undertaken it. When Collini's charge was put to him during his final illness, Berlin rejected it outright, observing that the provision of references 'has turned what were mere *belles-lettres* into scholarship'.[1] This remark displays Berlin's customary, and excessive, modesty and generosity, but it is answer enough, both to Collini and to Richardson, particularly if one adds that Berlin himself, when the necessary information was to hand, provided prodigious footnotes of his own – notably to 'The Originality of Machiavelli' and to *Vico and Herder*.[2] Nevertheless, in the case of a transcript of unscripted lectures, to print references as footnotes on the page would perhaps cause a particularly uncomfortable clash of atmospheres, and for this reason I have, this time, collected the references together here at the end of the text, identifying the passages to which they refer by page number and opening words so as not to disfigure the text with superior numerals or other symbols.

Most of the notes are references for quotations, or semi-quotations (see p. xiv above), but from time to time, when I happen to have it available, I have given a reference for a paraphrase. Ideally, perhaps, I should have provided references for all attributions of specific opinions: this is what Berlin himself attempted in the opening pages of 'The Originality of Machiavelli', where, analogously with the present case, a bewildering plethora of conflicting views is canvassed as a prelude to Berlin's own suggestions. However, to complete this task, even with the assistance of Berlin's surviving notes, would have taken many months at the very least, and I judged it better – here the epigraph from Dover comes in – to make the lectures available now, without such an exhaustive, and

[1] Letter from Pat Utechin, Berlin's secretary, to Henry Hardy, 12 December 1997.

[2] 'The Originality of Machiavelli' (1972) is included in *Against the Current: Essays in the History of Ideas* (London, 1979; New York, 1980) and in *The Proper Study of Mankind* (see p. ix above, note 2). *Vico and Herder: Two Studies in the History of Ideas* was published in London and New York in 1976.

perhaps disproportionate, scholarly apparatus, than to hold them up still further: it is already over thirty years, after all, since they were delivered. For the same reason I have not felt obliged to track down every last (semi-)quotation to its lair, as I did in the books of Berlin's essays that I published in his lifetime. Then, in the few instances in which I failed to find an apparent quotation, even with the assistance of experts in the relevant field, I removed the quotation marks and treated the passage as paraphrase, risking the charge of plagiarism in so doing (this procedure was endorsed by Berlin). Here, to avoid spending a great deal more time in searches many of which might well have proved fruitless, I have recorded that a few ostensible quotations are untraced. I shall be extremely grateful to anyone who can fill in the gaps, and in future impressions of this book I shall incorporate any information I receive. I fully expect to be put to shame by the experts.

The references that do appear below often depend on the generosity of other experts, to whom I am greatly indebted. Andrew Fairbairn has again been tireless in his support, and has ferreted out solutions that would certainly have eluded me if I had been left to my own devices. I have also been helped in specific individual cases by G. N. Anderson, Gunnar Beck, Prudence Bliss, Elfrieda Dubois, the late Patrick Gardiner, Gwen Griffith Dickson, Ian Harris, Roger Hausheer, Michael Inwood, Francis Lamport, James C. O'Flaherty, Richard Littlejohns, Bryan Magee, Alan Menhennet, T. J. Reed, David Walford, Robert Wokler, and others to whom I apologise for not keeping a better record of their assistance.

Page   *Reference*

Lecture 1

1   **Northrop Frye points out**
Northrop Frye, 'The Drunken Boat: The Revolutionary
Element in Romanticism', in Northrop Frye (ed.), *Romanti-
cism Reconsidered: Selected Papers from the English Institute*
(New York and London, 1963), pp. 1–25, at p. 1.

3   **'When Israel went out of Egypt'**
Psalm 114: 1, 3–4, 7.

4   **'Jovis omnia plena'**
Virgil, *Eclogue* 3. 60; cf. Aratus, *Phainomena* 2–4.

5   **The Baron Seillière**
Ernest Seillière, *Les Origines romanesques de la morale et de
la politique romantiques* (Paris, 1920), esp. section 2 of the
introduction (pp. 49 ff.), and chapter 1.

6   *plaisir de vivre*
[F. P. G.] Guizot, *Mémoires pour servir à l'histoire de mon
temps*, vol. 1 (Paris, 1858), p. 6: 'M. Talleyrand me disait un
jour: Qui n'a pas vécu dans les années voisines de 1789 ne sait
pas ce que c'est que le plaisir de vivre.'

11   **'a fiery mass of Life'**
Carlyle, 'The Hero as Prophet': p. 40 in Thomas Carlyle, *On
Heroes, Hero-Worship, & the Heroic in History*, ed. Michael
K. Goldberg and others (Berkeley etc., 1993).

'Dante's sublime Catholicism'
Carlyle, 'The Hero as Priest': ibid., p. 102.

13   **'good with good'**
See Hegel's *Vorlesungen über die Aesthetik*, in Georg
Wilhelm Friedrich Hegel, *Sämtliche Werke*, ed. Hermann
Glockner (Stuttgart, 1927–51), vols 12–14, *passim*, e.g. vol. 12,
p. 298, and vol. 14, pp. 529 and 554 [= G. W. F. Hegel,

Aesthetics: Lectures on Fine Art, trans. T. M. Knox (Oxford, 1975), pp. 220, 1196, 1216]. Not an exact quotation.

13   **'No, imbeciles!'**
Preface to Théophile Gautier, *Mademoiselle de Maupin*: p. 19 in the edition published in Paris in 1880.

14   **'emotion recollected in tranquillity'**
William Wordsworth, *Lyrical Ballads*, 2nd. ed. (London, 1800), preface, p. xxxiii.

Stendhal says
Stendhal, *Racine et Shakespeare* (Paris, 1823), beginning of chapter 3.

15   **'Le romantisme, c'est la révolution'**
This exact formulation not yet found in a printed source.

16   **'I speak everlastingly of myself'**
François-Auguste Chateaubriand, *Itinéraire de Paris à Jerusalem*, preface to the first edition: vol. 1, p. 71, line 25, in the edition by Emile Malakis (Baltimore and London, 1946).

Joseph Aynard says
Joseph Aynard, 'Comment définir le romantisme?', *Revue de littérature comparée* 5 (1925), 641–58.

Georg Lukács says
Georg Lukács, *The Historical Novel* (1937), trans. Hannah and Stanley Mitchell (London, 1962), esp. chapter 1, section 3 (pp. 63–88), 'The Classical Historical Novel in Struggle with Romanticism'.

17   **'la terre et les morts'**
This is a recurrent nationalist *leitmotiv* used by Barrès (and by later writers following his lead). A prominent occurrence is in the title of a lecture written for (but not delivered to) La Patrie Française: Maurice Barrès, *La Terre et les morts (Sur quelles réalités fonder la conscience française)* ([Ligue de] La Patrie Française, Troisième Conférence) (Paris, [1899]). The Ligue de la Patrie Française was a short-lived extra-parliamentary conservative association set up in December 1898, in the wake

of the Dreyfus affair, as a rival to the 'unpatriotic' *dreyfusard* Ligue des Droits de l'Homme.

the dead and the living and the yet unborn
Edmund Burke, *Reflections on the Revolution in France*: p. 147 in *The Writings and Speeches of Edmund Burke*, ed. Paul Langford (Oxford, 1981–   ), vol. 8, *The French Revolution*, ed. L. G. Mitchell (1989). Burke here describes society as 'a partnership not only between those who are living, but between those who are living, those who are dead, and those who are to be born'.

18   **'the starry heavens'**
Untraced.

A. O. Lovejoy
Arthur O. Lovejoy, 'The Meaning of Romanticism for the Historian of Ideas', *Journal of the History of Ideas* 2 (1941), 257–78.

19   **'[A]fter the discrimination'**
George Boas, 'Some Problems of Intellectual History', in [George] Boas and others, *Studies in Intellectual History* ([Baltimore], 1953), pp. 3–21, at p. 5.

20   **'One cannot get drunk'**
Paul Valéry, *Cahiers*, ed. Judith Robinson (Paris, 1973–4), vol. 2, pp. 1220–1 (from a notebook dated 1931–2).

'The whole pother'
Arthur Quiller-Couch, 'On the Terms Classical and Romantic', *Studies in Literature* [first series] (Cambridge, 1918), p. 94.

Lecture 2

26   **'A work of politics'**
Fontenelle, quoted without reference in Emery Neff, *The Poetry of History* (New York, 1947), p. 6; untraced in Fontenelle.

27   **'nature reduced to method'**
See René Rapin, *Les Réflexions sur la poétique de ce temps et*

sur les ouvrages des poètes anciens et modernes, preface: p. 9 in the edition by E. T. Dubois (Geneva, 1970).

27   **'Those RULES of old'**
Alexander Pope, *An Essay on Criticism*, lines 88–9.

28   **'noble simplicity' and 'calm grandeur'**
'edle Einfalt', 'stille Größe': Winckelmann, *Gedanken über die Nachahmung der griechischen Werke in der Malerei und Bildhauerkunst*: vol. 1, p. 30, in *Johann Winckelmanns Sämtliche Werke*, ed. Joseph Eiselein (Donaueschingen, 1825–9).

29   **'philosophy teaching by examples'**
[Henry St John, Viscount] Bolingbroke, *Letters on the Study and Use of History*, letter 2: vol. 2, p. 177, in *The Works of Lord Bolingbroke* (London, 1844). Bolingbroke says that he thinks he read the remark in Dionysius of Halicarnassus, and he is right (see *Ars rhetorica* 11. 2), except that the *Ars rhetorica* is no longer attributed to Dionysius. Pseudo-Dionysius attributes his version – 'History is philosophy from examples' – to Thucydides, but it is in fact a creative paraphrase of what Thucydides says at 1. 22. 3.

31   **when Montezuma said to Cortés**
Montesquieu, *De l'esprit des lois*, book 24, chapter 24.

38   **'Whoso wishes to grasp God'**
M. Aug. Gottlieb Spangenbergs Apologetische Schluß-Schrift ... (Leipzig and Görlitz, 1752 [photographically reprinted as Nikolaus Ludwig von Zinzendorf, *Ergänzungsbände zu den Hauptschriften*, ed. Erich Beyreuther and Gerhard Meyer (Hildesheim etc., 1964–85), vol. 3]), p. 181.

reason is a whore
See *Dr Martin Luther's sämmtliche Werke*, ed. Joh. Georg Plochmann and Johann Konrad Irmischer (Erlangen etc., 1826–57), vol. 16, pp. 142 and 144, and vol. 29, p. 241.

43   **Mendelssohn treats beauty**
Goethe, letter of 14 July 1770 to Hetzler the younger: part 4 (*Goethe's Briefe*), vol. 1, p. 238, lines 19 ff., in *Goethes Werke* (Weimar, 1887–1919).

44 **As man is made**
References to Hamann's works are to Johann Georg Hamann, *Sämtliche Werke*, ed. Joseph Nadler (Vienna, 1949–57) (hereafter W), by volume, page and line(s), thus: W ii 198.2–9 (of which this appears to be a paraphrase).

'What is this highly praised reason'
W iii 225.3–6.

'What one has felt'
Untraced.

45 **'In order to achieve'**
Goethe, *Aus meinem Leben: Dichtung und Wahrheit*, book 12: vol. 28, p. 109, lines 14–16, in *Goethes Werke* (see above, note to p. 43).

'All that a man undertakes'
ibid., p. 108, lines 25–8.

Lecture 3

48 **'Physiognomik'**
Johann Caspar Lavater, *Physiognomische Fragmente, zur Beförderung der Menschenkenntniß und Menschenliebe* (Leipzig and Winterthur, 1775–8), *passim* (Lavater defines the term as he uses it on p. 13). Modern words beginning 'physio(g)-nom-' (e.g. English 'physiognomy') derive, by an etymologically misleading telescoping of syllables, from Greek 'physio-gnomon-'; indeed a French edition, translator unnamed, which was overseen by Lavater and incorporates his revisions, is entitled *Essai sur la physiognomonie* (The Hague, [1781]–1803). *Physiognomik*, then, means 'nature-judgement'.

50 **'And their children wept'**
Blake, *The First Book of Urizen*, plate 28, lines 4–7. The text followed in these quotations from Blake is that to be found in *William Blake's Writings*, ed. G. E. Bentley, Jr (Oxford, 1978). References to this edition are given in parentheses, by volume and page, at the end of the relevant notes, thus: (i 282), the reference for this quotation.

50   **'A Robin Red breast in a Cage'**
'Auguries of Innocence', lines 5–6 (ii 1312).

'Children of the future Age'
Songs of Experience, plate 51 ('A Little GIRL Lost'), lines 1–4 (i 196).

'Art is the Tree of Life'
'Laocoon', aphorisms 17, 19 (i 665, 666).

52   **'Beware of those'**
[Denis] Diderot, *Salon de 1765*, ed. Else Marie Bukdahl and Annette Lorenceau (Paris, 1984), p. 47.

53   **'I did not reason'**
Rousseau, letter of 26 January 1762 to Chrétien-Guillaume de Lamoignon de Malesherbes: vol. 1, p. 1141, in Jean-Jacques Rousseau, *Oeuvres complètes*, ed. Bernard Gagnebin, Marcel Raymond and others (Paris, 1959–).

54   **the best of the sophists**
Untraced, but cf. Hamann, W ii 163.19.

55   **'Action, action'**
J. M. R. Lenz, 'Über Götz von Berlichingen': vol. 2, p. 638, in Jakob Michael Reinhold Lenz, *Werke und Briefe in Drei Bänden*, ed. Sigrid Damm (Munich/Vienna, 1987). A loose version.

63   *Schwerpunkt*
J. G. Herder, *Sämmtliche Werke*, ed. Bernhard Suphan (Berlin, 1877–1913), vol. 5, p. 509.

Lecture 4

68   **'The nature of things'**
Rousseau, *Émile*, book 2: vol. 4, p. 320 in op. cit. (note to p. 53 above).

69   **'a Tyger strongly chain'd'**
[Anthony Ashley Cooper, third Earl of] Shaftesbury, *An*

Inquiry concerning Virtue, or Merit, book 1, part 3, § 3: vol. 2, p. 55, in *Characteristicks of Men, Manners, Opinions, Times*, 2nd ed. ([London], 1714).

70 **'A paternalist government'**
Immanuel Kant, 'Über den Gemeinspruch: Das mag in der Theorie richtig sein, taugt aber nicht für die Praxis', section 2: vol. 8, p. 290, lines 35 ff., in *Kant's gesammelte Schriften* (Berlin, 1900–).

71 **'The man who stands in dependence on another'**
Kant, 'Von der Freyheit', in 'Bemerkungen zu den Beobach-tungen über das Gefühl des Schönen und Erhabenen': ibid., vol. 20, p. 94, lines 1–3.

75 **'turnspit'**
Kant, *Kritik der praktischen Vernunft*, part 1, book 1, chapter 3: ibid., vol. 5, p. 97, line 19.

80 **'The very circumstance'**
Schiller, 'Über das Erhabene': vol. 21, p. 50, lines 7–17, in *Schillers Werke*, Nationalausgabe (Weimar, 1943–).

84 **Schiller's fundamental view**
The reader should perhaps be warned that this is a very fore-shortened account of the complex (and not always pellucid) theory contained in Schiller's *Über die ästhetische Erziehung des Menschen* (1795).

88 **'At the mere mention'**
Quoted without reference, in Russian translation, in the article on Fichte in *Entsiklopedicheskii slovar'* (St Petersburg, 1890–1907), vol. 36, p. 50, col. 2; untraced in Fichte.

'A man's philosophy'
Fichte, *Erste Einleitung in die Wissenschaftslehre*: vol. 1, p. 434, in J. G. Fichte, *Sämtliche Werke*, ed. I. H. Fichte (Berlin, 1845–6) (hereafter SW).

89 **'We do not act'**
Fichte, *Die Bestimmung des Menschen*: SW, vol. 2, p. 263.

'I do not hunger'
ibid., p. 264.

89   **'I do not accept'**
ibid., p. 256 (loose).

'I am not determined'
ibid., pp. 264–5 (paraphrase).

'The world is the poem'
Josiah Royce, *The Spirit of Modern Philosophy: An Essay in the Form of Lectures* (Boston and New York, 1892), p. 162.

'To be free'
Quoted without reference in German ('Frei sein ist nichts – frei werden ist der Himmel'), loc. cit. (note to p. 88 above, 'At the mere mention'); untraced in Fichte.

90   **'Man should be and do something'**
Fichte, *Über das Wesen des Gelehrten* ..., lecture 4: SW, vol. 6, p. 383.

Lecture 5

95   **'Either you believe'**
Fichte, *Reden an die deutsche Nation*, No 7: SW, vol. 7, pp. 374–5.

104   **'Can the sacred be seized?'**
Untraced (paraphrase?).

           'I am always going home'
Untraced in this exact wording, which however probably derives from an exchange between the hero and Cyane in Novalis, *Heinrich von Ofterdingen*, part 2: vol. 1, p. 325, in Novalis, *Schriften*, ed. Richard Samuel and Paul Kluckhorn (Stuttgart, 1960–88). 'Where are we going then?' asks Heinrich; 'Always home,' Cyane replies. Cf. also this fragment: 'Philosophy is in essence homesickness. – *A longing everywhere to be at home.*' ibid., vol. 3, p. 434.

106   **'But Mr Rossetti'**
A probably apocryphal remark attributed to Jowett by Max

Beerbohm in the caption to a water-colour drawing of 1916 entitled 'A Remark by Benjamin Jowett'. The caption reads: 'The sole remark likely to have been made by Benjamin Jowett about the mural paintings at the Oxford Union. "And what were they going to do with the Grail when they found it, Mr Rossetti?" ' The drawing is at the Tate Gallery, London, and is reproduced as No 4 in Max Beerbohm, *Rossetti and his Circle* (London, 1922).

107   **'The spirit cheats us'**
Untraced (paraphrase?).

112   **'Romanticism is disease'**
Johann Paul Eckermann, *Gespräche mit Goethe in den letzten Jahren seines Lebens* (1836, 1848), 2 April 1829.

113   **'This is how one should live!'**
Paraphrase of ideas at the end of 'Charakteristik der Kleinen Wilhelmine', a section of Schlegel's *Lucinde*: vol. 5 (ed. Hans Eichner), p. 15, in *Kritische Friedrich-Schlegel-Ausgabe*, ed. Ernst Behler (Munich etc., 1958–).

115   **'You who come'**
The 'quotations' in this account of Tieck's plays, which appears to derive, at least in part, from George Brandes, *Main Currents in Nineteenth Century Literature*, vol. 2, *The Romantic School in Germany* (1873), English translation (London, 1902), pp. 153–5, are in fact a mixture of translation and paraphrase. For *Puss in Boots* see *Der gestiefelte Kater*, act 1, scene 2: p. 509, line 33, to p. 510, line 5, in Ludwig Tieck, *Schriften*, ed. Hans Peter Balmes and others (Frankfurt am Main, 1985–), vol. 6, *Phantasus*, ed. Manfred Frank; for the last remark about this play, 'But this is the flouting ...', perhaps cf. act 3, scene 3 (p. 546, lines 21–3). The play in which Scaramouche ('Skaramuz' in German) is a character is *Die verkehrte Welt*. For the passages referred to here see act 2, scene 3: p. 588, lines 2–29, in the edition of *Phantasus* cited above; the last remark, 'You must cease ...', and the following comments may derive from Brandes' translations of passages from act 3, scene 5 (p. 612, lines 5–7, and p. 622, lines 5–9 and 24–7).

Lecture 6

120 **to dissect is to murder**
'We murder to dissect': William Wordsworth in 'The Tables Turned' (1798).

122 **'The roots of life'**
Untraced.

'The romantic art'
Friedrich Schlegel, Athenaüms-Fragmente: vol. 2 (ed. Hans Eichner), p. 183, in op. cit. (note to p. 113 above).

124 **Burke's great images**
loc. cit. (note to p. 17 above).

'is not a mere factory'
Adam H. Müller, *Die Elemente der Staatskunst*, ed. Jakob Baxa (Jena, 1922), vol. 1, p. 37.

127 **'Sonate, que me veux-tu?'**
Attributed to Fontenelle in Rousseau's article 'Sonate' in the *Encyclopédie*; Rousseau revised the article for his *Dictionnaire de musique* (Paris, 1768).

128 **'Il arriva'**
Jean-François Marmontel, *Polymnie* vii 100–5: pp. 108–9 in James M. Kaplan, *Marmontel et 'Polymnie'* (Oxford, 1984; = *Studies on Voltaire and the Eighteenth Century*, ed. H. T. Mason, 229) [or, in another subdivision, *Polymnie* vi [100–5]: p. 278 in *Oeuvres posthumes de Marmontel* (Paris, 1820)].

129 **'What man, exhausted'**
Germaine de Staël, *Lettres sur les ouvrages et le caractère de J. J. Rousseau* (Paris, 1788; photographic reprint, Geneva, 1979), letter 5 (p. 88).

music 'shows us all the movements of our spirit'
Wackenroder, 'Die Wunder der Tonkunst', published posthumously in *Phantasien über die Kunst, für Freunde der Kunst*, ed. Ludwig Tieck (Hamburg, 1799), p. 156: vol. 1, p. 207, lines 35–6, in Wilhelm Heinrich Wackenroder, *Sämtliche Werke*

und Briefe, ed. Silvio Vietta and Richard Littlejohns (Heidelberg, 1991).

'The composer reveals'
Arthur Schopenhauer, *Die Welt als Wille und Vorstellung*, vol. 1, § 52: vol. 2, p. 307, lines 29–31, in *Sämtliche Werke*, ed. Arthur Hübscher, 2nd ed. (Wiesbaden, 1946–50).

130 **'When storms rage'**
Untraced.

131 **Schiller's bent twig**
In the lectures Berlin ascribed this image to Diderot, but I have substituted Schiller, to whom he ascribes it in essays he later published himself. I have not been able to find the bent twig in either author, though the view of nationalism it encapsulates is present in Schiller's *Geschichte des Abfalls der vereinigten Niederlande von der spanischen Regierung* (1788). Could Berlin have invented it?

132 **'The Ancients scarcely knew'**
François-Auguste Chateaubriand, *Génie du christianisme* (Paris, 1802), part 2, book 3, chapter 9 (vol. 2, p. 159, in this first edition).

'L'obéissance est douce'
From the unpublished 'Poëme sur l'orgeuil' (1846) by an unnamed member of a Satanist group, quoted by Louis Maigron, *Le Romantisme et les moeurs* (Paris, 1910), p. 188.

133 **'Forward, forward'**
Not a quotation from Goethe's *Faust*; perhaps a paraphrase of the Faustian spirit. There are echoes at, e.g., part 2, lines 11,433 ff. 'Never ask the moment . . .' is a reference to Faust's wager with the devil: part 1, lines 1,699 ff., and cf. part 2, lines 11,574–86 (Faust's last speech).

'Apart he stalked'
Byron, *Child Harold's Pilgrimage*, Canto I. 6.

'There was in him'
Lara, Canto I. 18, lines 313, 315, 345–6.

133 **'My Spirit walked not'**
Manfred, act 2, scene 2, lines 51 ff.

138 **'*Nature Methodiz'd*'**
Pope, loc. cit. (note to p. 27 above).

141 **'tepid water on the tongue'**
Hölderlin, *Hyperion*, vol. 1, book 1: vol. 2, p. 118, in
Hölderlin, *Sämtliche Werke*, ed. Norbert v. Hellingrath,
Friedrich Seebass and Ludwig v. Pigenot (Berlin, 1943–).

142 **'Man does not desire happiness'**
Friedrich Nietzsche, *Götzen-Dämmerung*, 'Sprüche und
Pfeile', No 12: vol. 6. 3, p. 55, in Nietzsche, *Werke*, ed.
Giorgio Colli and Mazzino Montinari (Berlin, 1967–).

INDEX

Compiled by Douglas Matthews

action: Fichte on, 88–90
aesthetics: and reason, 22; and nature, 27–8; *see also* art
Alembert, Jean Le Rond d', 39
Alexander the Great, 27, 37
alienation, 71
allegory, 101–2
Aristotle, 3, 27, 37, 138; *Nicomachean Ethics*, 4
Arnold, Gottfried, 36
art: purpose of, 13–14; and romanticism, 18; and depiction of nature, 26–8; and creative imagination, 51, 119; and aesthetics, 58–60; and notion of belonging, 61–2; Schelling on life in, 98–9; and profundity, 103–4
Aynard, Joseph, 16

Babbitt, Irving, 130
Bach, Johann Sebastian, 35, 36n
Bacon, Francis, 137
Balzac, Honoré de: *Le Chef d'oeuvre inconnu*, 13
Batteux, abbé Charles, 51, 58
beauty: objective ideals of, 28
Becker, Carl: *The Heavenly City of the Eighteenth-Century Philosophers*, 32

Beethoven, Ludwig van, 13, 129–30
belief: Hume's doubts on, 32–3
Bellow, Saul: *Herzog*, x
belonging: Herder on notion of, 58, 60–3, 66
Bergin, Thomas Goddard and Max Harold Fisch, xivn
Bergson, Henri, 42, 88, 98
Berlioz, Hector, 18
Bernini, Giovanni Lorenzo, 27
Berz, I., 36n
Besterman, Theodore, xivn
Bible: and thought framework, 3; and pietism, 36; effect on Hamann, 40
Blake, William, 18, 49–50
Boas, George, 19–20
Boehme, Jacob, 90, 105
Brunetière, Ferdinand, 15
Büchner, Georg, 17; *The Death of Danton*, 12
Buffon, Georges Louis Leclerc, comte de, 38
Burke, Edmund, 90n, 124, 126
Butler, Joseph, ix
Byron, George Gordon, 6th Baron: influence, 8; romanticism, 18, 131–4, 146

exploitation: as evil, 71, 73
expressionism, 58

Fascism, 139, 145–6
Ferguson, Adam, 90n
Fichte, Johann Gottlieb: social
    origins, 38; doctrines, 88–91,
    99, 102, 119, 139, 143; on self,
    93–5; speeches to German
    nation, 95–7; in Jena, 113;
    economics, 126
folk song, 59–60, 99
Fontanes, Louis de, 129
Fontenelle, Bernard le Bovier de,
    24, 26, 30, 127
France: *philosophes* in, 6; subdues
    and humiliates Germany, 35,
    39–40, 109; German hostility
    to, 49–51; romantics in, 134,
    147; *see also* Enlightenment, the
Francke, August Hermann, 36
Frederick II (The Great), King of
    Prussia, 57, 70, 131, 140–1
freedom, 73–4, 79, 88–91, 113,
    139
Freemasonry, 47
French Revolution: influence on
    romantic movement, 6–7, 103,
    109; Carlyle on, 11; Kant
    welcomes, 77; attempts to
    explain, 107; consequences,
    109–10
Freud, Sigmund, 119
friendship: Aristotle on, 4
Frye, Northrop, xii, 1, 16

Galiani, abbé Ferdinand, 39
Gardiner, Patrick Lancaster, xv
Gautier, Théophile, 13, 19
generosity: Kant sees as vice, 75
Genghis Khan, 35
genius: Diderot on, 52

Gentz, Friedrich von, 15
Germany: and origins of
    romanticism, 6, 12, 34, 38, 57,
    130–1, 146; and economic self-
    sufficiency, 14; disunity and
    isolation, 34–8; resentment of
    France and French, 39–40,
    49–51, 109; *Sturm und Drang*
    drama, 55–7; and folk song,
    59–60; and national identity,
    60–1, 91–2, 95–7; and romantic
    hero, 84; Greek influence on,
    87, 105; and creative nature, 95
Gibbon, Edward, 29
Gluck, Christoph Willibald, 128
Goethe, Johann Wolfgang von:
    friends, 8; on romanticism and
    romantics, 14, 111–12; opposes
    German provincialism, 38;
    social background, 38; and
    Hamann, 40, 45; on
    Mendelssohn, 43; on
    anthropomorphism, 104;
    shocked at F. Schlegel's
    Lucinde, 113; questionable
    romanticism, 132–3; *Faust*, 112,
    122, 132; *Hermann und
    Dorothea*, 112; *Die
    Wahlverwandtschaften*, 112;
    Werther, 57, 82; *Wilhelm
    Meister*, 93, 110–11
Gogol, Nikolay Vasil'evich: 'The
    Nose', 135
good, the: notions of, 23–5
Greeks (ancient): thought
    framework, 3–4; on tragedy, 12;
    understanding of, 62, 64–6;
    influence on German romantics,
    87, 121–2
Grimm, Friedrich Melchior,
    Baron von, 39

romanticism, 68; moral philosophy, 69–75, 77, 81, 86, 139–40; influence on Schiller, 78, 80, 83, 85; and primacy of will, 78, 97; and nationalism, 92; on self, 93; 'An Answer to the Question: "What is Enlightenment?" ', 70
Kemal Pasha (Atatürk), 10
Kierkegaard, Søren, 41, 124
Kleist, Christian Ewald, 38
Klinger, Friedrich Maximilian von: *Sturm und Drang*, 55; *The Twins*, 55–6
knowledge: and Enlightenment, 21–3, 25; virtue and, 25, 118, 120; as instrument, 88–9

La Mettrie, Julien Offray de, 24
La Popelinière, Madame de (*née* Deshayes), 30
Lamartine, Alphonse Marie Louis de, 134
language: Hamann on, 44; Herder on, 60–1
Laocoon, 79–80
Lavater, Johann Caspar, 48
law, 125–6
Lawrence, David Herbert: *Lady Chatterley's Lover*, 113–14
Leibniz, Gottfried Wilhelm von, 34, 46
Leisewitz, Johann Anton: *Julius von Tarent*, 56
Lenz, Jakob Michael Reinhold, 54, 67
Lessing, Gotthold Ephraim, 38; *Minna von Barnhelm*, 83–4
List, Friedrich, 126
Locke, John, 49, 89

Louis XVI, King of France, 6–7
Lovejoy, Arthur Oncken, 18–20, 134
Lukács, Georg, 16
Luther, Martin, 34, 38
Lutheranism, 35–6

Mably, abbé Gabriel Bonnot de, 8, 39
Macaulay, Thomas Babington, Baron, 137
Machiavelli, Niccolò, 8
Mahler, Gustav, 123
Maine de Biran, François Pierre Gonthier, 97
Maistre, Joseph de, 125
Marmontel, Jean-François, 128
martyrdom, 10
Marx, Karl: Greek influence on, 87; and class war, 107
Marxism: on romanticism, 15; theodicy, 110
Mendelssohn, Moses, 43, 45
Metternich, Clemens Wenzel Lothar, Prince, 15
Michelet, Jules, 17
Mill, James, 137, 139
Milton, John, 79
miracles, 47
Molière, Jean Baptiste Poquelin de: *Le Misanthrope*, 83
Montesquieu, Charles Louis de Secondat, baron de: beliefs, 30–1, 33, 41, 76; social background, 39
Montezuma, 31
morality: Kant on, 69–75
Moravian Brotherhood, 38
Morellet, abbé André, 39
Mozart, Wolfgang Amadeus, 130; *Don Giovanni*, 122–4

THE A. W. MELLON LECTURES IN THE FINE ARTS
Delivered at the National Gallery of Art, Washington, D.C.